British Railways Illustrated Summer Special No.2

IRWELL PRESS

CONTENTS

Copyright:- Irwell Press 1994
All rights reserved.
ISBN 1-871608-64-3

Readers can subscribe to British Railways Illustrated(published monthly) for six or twelve issues at a time. The cost for six issues is £13.20 inclusive of postage and packing whilst twelve issues are charged at £26.40. Overseas subscribers should add the cost of surface/air mail. All enquiries to SELECT SUBSCIPTIONS LTD. Northbridge Road, Berkhampstead, Herts, HP4 1ST. All remittances should be made payable to:- IRWELL PRESS MAGAZINES LTD., Telephone: 0442 876661; FAX: 0442 872279

Irwell Press,
15 Lovers Lane, Grasscroft,
Oldham 0L4 4DP
Printed by Amadeus Press, Huddersfield

Cover: Bournemouth for sun and the sea. Waterloo on 6th June 1951.
Rear cover: West Country summer - 5573 at Kingsbridge, 29th August 1959. Photo: Terry Nicholls.
Title Page: 62739 THE BADSWORTH on station pilot duties, shunting stock at Scarborough (Londesboro' Road) in the 1950s. Photo: Ken Hoole, coll. N.Stead.
Frontispiece: Up Boat Train at Folkestone Junction in October 1958 hauled by Merchant Navy Class No. 35015 Rotterdam Lloyd. Photo: R C Riley
Right: Never able to resist photographing trains, even (especially?) when on holiday - Stephen Gradidge's portrait of the Torrington bay at Halwill Junction in July 1963.

Welcome to the second **British Railways Illustrated Summer Special.** Another black and white trip to the seaside for sand, sun and steam. The holiday theme tends to dominate though one eye, at least, has to be kept upon the balance and spread of topic and geography.

Thirties File is a popular regular from the pages of the magazine and what better place to celebrate than the bracing east coast at Scarborough. Roads jammed with cars now characterise such summer Saturdays, where once the trains, from every conceivable place of origin, had backed up behind each other for miles. Evening excursions from Leeds and the West Riding could take nearly *four hours* to cover the journey (York to Scarborough was normally only an hour), stopping at every signal as the congestion reached almost unimaginable proportions.

The Very Last One commemorates the end of Britain's holiday train *par excellence*. The Atlantic Coast Express in September 1964. A somewhat poignant tale though the sombre tone is relieved by some scenes from the train's days of glory. D.W. Winkworth was there on that final day recording the to and fro and the last rites, taking some crumb of melancholy comfort from the fact that the very last engine, though a grubby BR Class 5, at least carried an ancient Southern name - MELISANDE....

Diesel Dawn is a regular feature in BRILL and *Parsifal* recalls in illuminating and often highly amusing fashion the early (often sore in the extreme) trials of introducing The New Order. In classic and riveting insider style the writer brings to life unimaginable goings on - double headed Deltics (teaching Wagner a thing or two about putting on a show) diesels bursting into flame like the funeral of some early barbarian chieftain and the idiosyncrasies and idiocies of the changeover steam to diesel - a time of great tribulation. One wag (and the idea was not universally taken *entirely* as a joke) proposed that some of the worst Type 2s have their tops removed and the innards taken out to serve as high capacity coal trains - hauled by an Austerity 2-8-0, naturally enough.

The Swinton and Knottingley Joint is recalled in **Summer Saturday on the S & K.** Peter Cookson, fired by the discovery of ancient dust covered notes in his loft, brings us a summer Saturday in the 1950s with a series of observations and descriptions of that achingly nostalgic time when to perch oneself by a lineside on any half decent piece of railway in Britain brought an endless procession of steam, in bewildering and delightful variety.

The Thanet Belle, whilst it was unlikely to have carried any of the hordes bound 'for the beach' at Margate and Ramsgate, continues (if slightly under false pretences) the bucket and spade theme, and what better gateway to Summer Saturdays in the West than **Newton Abbot and Moretonhampstead?**

A little known type of excursion, hardly ever recorded in notes or photographs in the railway press, was the peculiarly Scottish institution of the Orange Walks. In **Orange Walks Specials,** familiar **British Railways Illustrated** contributors, Paul Anderson and W.A.C. Smith, bring us Protestant Order mass marches, banners and bands and half of the engine types (or more) to be seen north of the border in the 1950s.

It's So Bracing!

You'll remember those black and white days

The Way It Was. The Southern Railway's Atlantic Coast Express on Honiton Bank. The view is a publicity shot taken by the Southern Railway for use in its Paris office where, no doubt, the absence of the usual King Arthur 4-6-0 (827 was an S15 mixed traffic locomotive) would go unobserved. *Photograph by arrangement John Tatchell.*

THE VERY LAST ONE

BY D.W.WINKWORTH

Three decades have passed since we said farewell to the Atlantic Coast Express - known to most simply as "The ACE". Can it really be thirty years since we paid our last respects? Alas, the calendar confirms it to be so, for on Saturday, 5th September, 1964, the last journeys of this famous train were made, carrying holidaymakers from London to Ilfracombe, Torrington, Bude and Padstow and places in between and back again.

On summer Saturdays the Atlantic Coast Express was a multi-portioned train and in 1964 there were two down parts and three up to London, although none of these ran to the faster schedule of other weekdays. It was for this reason that many of the aficionados and cognoscenti or just plain lovers of the train decided to take a farewell by travelling on the down service on Friday, 4th September (already the up working had succumbed to diesel hydraulic traction). In theory there must have been a good few grandmother's funerals taking place at Salisbury or west thereof that day! Some elected to travel to Salisbury and then back by the up train, others decided to go as far as Exeter and one or two right through to the very end of the line - Padstow.

The passing of the 38-year old title might have become something akin to an Irish wake but, in the event, there was an air of expectancy that September morning, almost as though this was the inaugural run of an express service. The platform barriers were accordingly opened a full three quarters of an hour before departure time, to admit those admirers who had already gathered. It was not one of the once-familiar M7 0-4-4Ts that brought in the empty stock but BR 3MT 2-6-2T No.82016. The 13 coaches - one over the maximum load laid down - were gleaming and complete with roofboards bearing the title THE ATLANTIC COAST EXPRESS. The cleaners at Nine Elms shed, no doubt aided by their Weaver Steam Jenny machines for cleaning wheels and motions (see BRILL 3.6 and subsequent correspondence for the background to this unusual apparatus) had done their work well in turning out as spick and span a Merchant Navy as had ever powered the train, in No.35022 HOLLAND-AMERICA LINE, complete with headboard carrying the proud name. The assembled company took their seats in anticipation: some looked forward to their last lunch on the train, others had a drink in mind, the recorders were ready with notebooks and stopwatches for the last fast run while

Merchant Navy Pacific 35022 HOLLAND-AMERICA LINE about to resume with the down Atlantic Coast Express on 4th September 1964, after taking water at Salisbury. Photograph D.W. Winkworth.

many were just content to savour the occasion. Ordinary travellers were perhaps a little bemused at this unusual activity.

Driver Sibley of Salisbury did his best to dampen down the wilder expectations of a record run before, promptly at 11 o'clock, he opened the regulator to start the train on its way. Good acceleration was made by 35022 out towards Vauxhall, only to be rewarded with a double yellow, a yellow and then an unblinking red aspect of successive colour light signals. The train came to a halt opposite Nine Elms goods depot but fortunately it was nothing more serious than a signal failure and the handsignalman with his flags quickly explained the position so that the train was soon on the move again. Even so, Clapham Junction was passed three and a half minutes late but determined running brought the speed up to 70 mph by Surbiton, where a lady photographer recorded the event on film. Time was steadily regained as the train sped westward so that by the time Worting Junction was passed the arrears, save for a few seconds, had been wiped off. Keeping to the speed limit driver

Sibley reined in HOLLAND-AMERICA LINE stopwatch brigade with a sprinkling of 'eighties' - the highest being 86 mph - and came to a stop in Salisbury station two minutes early, in the finest traditions of enginemanship on the ACE. When the signal stop was taken into consideration this equated to a net time of 74 1/2 minutes for the 83.7 miles, an average speed of 67.4 mph - a fine effort with 470 tons.

At Salisbury there was always a change of driver so Exmouth Junction's F. Turner took over, one with a reputation for good running. A punctual public timetable departure was made (a minute in advance of the working book) and 35022 soon got into its stride again. The summit at Semley

WATERLOO - SALISBURY (11.00 Atlantic Coast Express). 4 Sept 1964 35022 HOLLAND AMERICA LINE. Load 13 coaches (440/470 tons)					
Miles	Point	Gradient	Schedule	Actual	mph	dbhp
0.00	WATERLOO		00.00	00.00	-	-
	Signal stop					
3.90	Clapham Jcn	1/20358F	07.00	10.26	40	359
9.80	New Malden	1/1705R		16.57	65	1209
13.30	Hampton Court Jcn	1/2609F	18.00	20.02	72	1174
24.30	WOKING	1/1084R		28.56	74	1219
31.00	MP.31	1/312R		34.35	70	1502
39.80	Winchfield	1/2338R		41.37	78	1328
47.80	BASINGSTOKE	1/761R		47.52	68	967
50.30	Worting Jcn	1/241R	50.00	50.11	65	1440
55.60	Overton	1/453R		54.31	80	2220
66.40	ANDOVER JCN	1/388F		62.31	84	468
72.70	Grateley	1/275R		67.33	71	1380
78.20	Porton	1/571F		71.53	84	1239
					86	
83.70	SALISBURY	1/216F	80.00	78.07	-	

West Country Pacifics 34106 LYDFORD and 34079 141 SQUADRON entering Templecombe with the 10.28am Exeter Central - Waterloo train on 5th September 1964. BR standard Class 5 4-6-0 73049 waits in the background with stock for a Somerset & Dorset service. *Photograph D.W. Winkworth.*

was breasted at 60 mph and then came one of those dramatic increases in speed that this switchback route encouraged, so that Gillingham was passed at 89 mph and the regular travellers were not disappointed in experiencing that peculiar pat on the backside, on passing under the bridge at the eastern end of the station, which over the years they had come to expect at that point. Down into the dip after Buckhorn Weston tunnel the speed rose to 88 mph and then tailed off to 64 mph at the 113 1/2 milepost summit, to be followed by a full 90 mph at Sherborne. Consequently Yeovil Junction was cleared in 37 minutes 8 seconds against the 39 minutes allowed. Progress was such that another minute was gained to Axminster and, as the train was running about four minutes early, driver Turner eased off, striking no more than 80 mph below Axminster. This caused some momentum to be lost for the attack on Honiton bank, where speed dropped to a minimum of 37 mph. A sharp allowance for the final stretch resulted in a quarter of a minute overrun on the 73 minutes scheduled for the arrival at Sidmouth Junction, though it was still before the time of the public timetable. It seems the driver had momentarily overlooked that he had an extra coach on and had taken matters just a mite too easily. For the run into Exeter Central the passengers were

The 10.35am from Waterloo has light Pacific 34089 602 SQUADRON in charge, romping up the grade from Templecombe on 5th September 1964. The nameplate and plaque have been cleaned for the occasion. *Photograph D.W. Winkworth.*

treated to an 88 mph maximum. At Exeter 35022 came off and the train divided into Ilfracombe and Padstow sections of which the latter was taken forward by 34015 EXMOUTH.

For the final day, the Saturday, this author took up his pitch slightly west of Templecombe to witness the passing of all five trains. So numerous were

the photographers, observers and trainspotters that they appeared to outnumber the ordinary passengers at the station. At Templecombe there was, of course, the added attraction of the Somerset and Dorset route crossing under the west of England main line and making cross-platform connections at the station. The 9.30am

Exmouth - Waterloo train had a sobering effect on the crowd because it was handled by D831 MONARCH, one of the diesel hydraulic machines which were to displace steam on the route. However, No.35012 UNITED STATES LINES on the 9 o'clock Waterloo - Sidmouth and Exmouth service cheered things up considerably, as did 34106 LYDFORD and 34079 141 SQUADRON, double heading on the 10.28 Exeter Central - Waterloo train which had originated as separate parts from Plymouth and Ilfracombe.

In due course the first ACE of the last day appeared, the 10.35am Waterloo to Padstow and Bude, with 34089 602 SQUADRON climbing resolutely up to the summit at milepost 113 1/2, to be followed by the final down ACE which, as on the previous day, was in the charge of 35022 and again made up to 13 coaches - though lacking the engine headboard. There was not too long to wait to see the first of the three up ACEs, the 10.30am from Ilfracombe, the 12.30pm off Exeter Central. With no more than ten coaches, Merchant Navy No.35009 SHAW SAVILL appeared to have matters well in hand and one could sense the power as it accelerated mightily downhill towards the station, with its whistle wailing a long warning of its approach, and beyond down the dead straight dip into the bosom of

The Ilfracombe ACE (12.30pm ex-Exeter Central) running down towards Templecombe in charge of Merchant Navy 35009 SHAW SAVILL on 5th September 1964. There is a route disc missing - there should be a second one in the centre of the buffer beam. *Photograph D.W. Winkworth.*

Blackmore Vale, followed by a surge up into the blackness of Buckhorn Weston tunnel. It was the rapid fluctuations in gradient, and consequently speed, over this racing ground that many found so thrilling. Constant high speed with diesel traction is pretty small beer in comparison!

Hotly pursuing 35009 was 34093 SAUNTON with the 10.48am Torrington/Bude service (12.43pm from Exeter Central), the second of the

Modified West Country No.34093 SAUNTON, needing attention from the cleaning gang, accelerating down towards Templecombe with the Torrington ACE (12.43pm from Exeter Central) on 5th September 1964. *Photograph D.W. Winkworth.*

The Very Last One: BR Standard 5MT 4-6-0 73085 MELISANDE in filthy condition puts out a smoke screen to add to the gloom, the sun having veiled its face, as it heads the 11am from Padstow (2.10pm ex-Exeter Central) on the descent to Templecombe on 5th September 1964. No doubt by the time the train had been due to leave Exeter the motive power authorities were running a little short of power and it is something of a shame that the last ACE from Padstow could not have been handled throughout by a thoroughbred SR locomotive. (The train was diagrammed for a Merchant Navy during the height of the summer and a light Pacific for the last few weeks of the season). 73085, however, was not without some claim to a Southern pedigree, having originally been delivered to Stewarts Lane for the working of the Victoria - Ramsgate services, transferring to the South Western after the 1959 electrification of the main lines in Kent. *Photograph D.W. Winkworth.*

up ACE trains. There was some time to elapse before the third one was to come and in the interval the Plymouth - Brighton train passed through in charge of BR Standard 4-6-0 No.73162, followed by the noon departure from Ilfracombe (the 1.50pm from Exeter Central) for Waterloo drawn by large Pacific 35007 ABERDEEN COMMONWEALTH.

Cloud covered the sun for the final act, the 11 o'clock from Padstow plus through coaches from Bude, making up nine coaches in all, and when it appeared, there at the head was a BR 5MT 4-6-0. Fortunately it was No.73085, which carried the surrogate name MELISANDE, one which a Southern King Arthur had carried for many years and which locomotive had doubtless toiled up and down these western banks over many years with numerous holiday makers in its trains. So it was fitting that one of those old names should be associated with THE VERY LAST ONE. We went home as contented as could be in the circumstances, acknowledging that the old train had bowed out well!

Merchant Navy 4-6-2 No. 35022 HOLLAND-AMERICA LINE climbing past Templecombe with the 11am ACE from Waterloo on 5th September 1964. *Photograph D.W. Winkworth.*

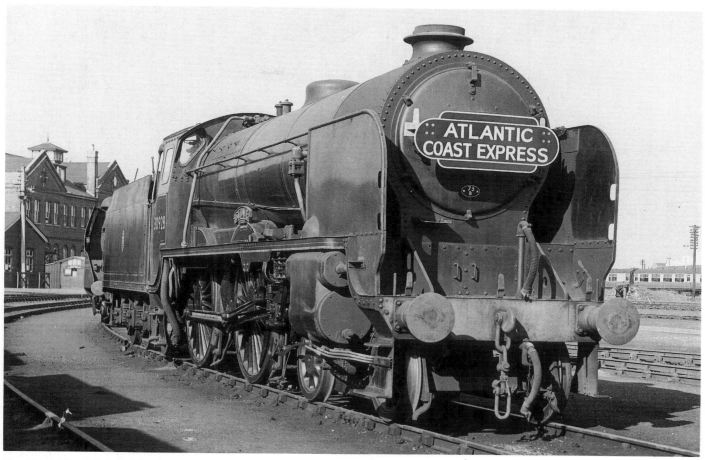

On show at Eastleigh 1: Schools class 4-4-0 30928 STOWE in 1952 with a version of the ACE headboard (see the Merchant Navy Pacific behind in BRILL 2.5, similarly adorned). *Photograph by arrangement John Tatchell.*

On show at Eastleigh 2: Lord Nelson 4-6-0 30857 LORD HOWE with the 'sausage' style board. The occasion is the same day as STOWE. *Photograph by arrangement John Tatchell.*

SUMMER SATURDAY
ON THE S & K

A photogenic review of a little-known cross-country main line.

Peter Cookson.

The idea for this article arose in rather an odd way. Some time ago I was going through a sheaf of papers which had been temporarily stored in the loft many years earlier when, quite by accident, I came upon an old examination paper, taken some forty years ago. It was the Northern Universities' Joint Board Scholarship Physics paper which I had sat in 1953 as part of my 'A' Level examination. For a few moments I paused to read through the questions again, just to see whether I could remember anything of them. Judging by the fairly confident ticks in the margin of the paper I had obviously fancied my chances with the Compound Pendulum, Newton's Gravitation Law and Millikan's Oil Drop experiment, but the ticks for questions on the Doppler Effect and Stoke's Law were a little more diffident. At any rate, I appeared to have had a go at the requisite five questions but it did not take me long to conclude that forty years was more than enough time to forget them almost completely - indeed I now hardly even remember taking the examination.

And then came the surprise: just as I was about to put the paper back again (I hadn't the heart to throw it away) I noticed, written on the back page in pencil, a full list of the trains which had passed through Pontefract (Baghill) Station on some particular Saturday morning shortly after June 23rd 1953. I have only a vague memory of the event but I imagine that watching and recording the trains go by must have been my way of relaxing after the rigours of the 'A' Level examination; however, it remained a one-off exercise until 1957. In April of that year I received, as a birthday present, five volumes of "Locomotive and Train Working in the Latter Part of the Nineteenth Century" by E.L. Ahrons; I enjoyed these books immensely and it occurred to me that it might be a good idea to make notes of locomotive and train working in my own neck of the woods, for anyone who might be interested in them at some time in the future. This good intention lasted some three or four weeks in that summer until overtaken once again by indolence. This article is based mainly on those observations. I should mention here that it is not intended to give any account of the history of the Swinton and Knottingley Joint Line of the Mid-

For me this picture says it all and captures perfectly those days by the lineside in the 1950s. This is the location where the observations were made - just to the south of Cobbler's Lane bridge on the public footpath which ran along the lineside to the lane over the bridge. In those days I would only have had (maybe) eight exposures available in the camera (twelve at the most) so I could only expect to photograph about a quarter of the trains during a morning by the lineside and I evidently decided to let this one go by - after all, it was only another B16! Fortunately my friend Peter Tait didn't mind my being in the way and decided to take the photograph - and I'm so glad he did, for he secured the sort of scene which was the very quintessence of those Saturdays by the line. Class B16/3 No. 61464 (50A:York) appears to be heading a southbound relief, but I do not recognize the tablet number 906. *(Peter Tait 15-6-57)*

land and North Eastern Railways, nor to give any detailed analysis of its traffic patterns, but simply to try to convey something of the "flavour" of the line on summer Saturdays in the 1950s.

For the benefit of readers who are not familiar with the line I should perhaps explain that the Swinton and Knottingley Joint was essentially a "cut-off" which shortened the journey from Sheffield to York via Normanton or Doncaster, by striking off from the North Midland main line at Wath Road junction near Swinton, to join the North Eastern at Ferrybridge, near Knottingley. There were stations at Bolton-on-Dearne, Frickley, Moorthorpe and South Kirby, Ackworth and Pontefract, with Pontefract much the most important

town on the line. The Wath curve and the curve from Mexborough West Junction fed the Great Central services into the S&K line at Dearne Junction, which was an important double junction.

One of the problems that the amateur linesider faced on summer Saturdays, in trying to identify some of the specials and reliefs that came along, was the fact that they might have come from two or three different directions at Dearne Junction, and when trains ran late or 9out of path they would be seen down the line out of order. In similar fashion, for southbound trains coming from Milford Junction, late running of some might well bring them through Pontefract out of order. For these reasons some of the identities of trains

Looking back towards the town from a little higher up the footpath the 9.08 a.m. train to York (8.20 a.m. ex Sheffield, Victoria) leaves Baghill behind class D11 No. 62666 ZEEBRUGGE during June 1957 but it may not have been on the occasion of the June 29th observations in Table 3. The destination of this train in summer was sometimes York and sometimes Scarborough. The Darnall D11s were very active on this train at the time and I took quite a few pictures of them. The station is located beyond the overbridge in the background and on the wooded hill behind All Saint's Church tower lie the remains of Pontefract Castle.

given here must count as "best guesses".

The observations were made at or near Pontefract (Baghill) Station which was one of three in the town; the other two were on the L&Y lines at the other side of town. Mainly through its history and geography, Pontefract never became a railway centre as such but there was much of railway interest here. Roughly speaking, the L&Y lines supplied local needs with stopping services to Leeds, Wakefield and Goole (and earlier to Doncaster) while the S&K line, part of the NE - SW trunk route at the time, supplied a variety of middle and long-distance services, with the result that, all-in-all, Pontefract was quite well served, but not in a concentrated way. The 1953 observations were made from a public footpath near to the Cobbler's Lane bridge to the north of the station which, at that time, was pleasantly rural but is now covered with housing. Because of the hilly nature of the town this was about the only place where traffic on both the L&Y lines and the S&K line could be seen and it used to be a favourite vantage point for local enthusiasts. The surviving record shows that I recorded the locomotive number, shed code and the number of coaches in the train, but not the train's identity, except in the case of those main line expresses carrying coach destination boards. It evidently did not occur to me to make a note of the smokebox tablet numbers of the Saturdays Only holiday trains. It has proved to be an interesting exercise to try to identify these so long after the event, but I can-

not, and do not claim that these are entirely free from error.

In Table 1, 1954 has been chosen as an illustrative year to indicate the general shape of Saturday services at Pontefract (Baghill); bracketed times indicate the approximate passing times of non-stopping trains which have not

been obtained from working timetables but interpolated from the public timetable - unfortunately, I do not have ready access to working timetables.

Table 2 shows the 1953 observations while Tables 3 and 4 are those made in 1957. In all cases a single consecutive list was made but I have rearranged these into separate up and down trains with times staggered to give some idea of the distribution of trains throughout the day. For various reasons only the morning trains figure in these observations. As far as the photographs are concerned, I had no suitable camera before 1955 so, although I have some box camera stills from before this time, lineside pictures were not possible in 1953. Some pictures were taken on the 1957 occasions; however, I have chosen to illustrate the article with photographs taken over a longer period in the interests of variety.

Table 1 shows the general shape of services over the S&K line which stayed more or less the same over the whole decade of the 1950s and into the early 1960s. I suppose it is fair to say that in the 1950s the core service was the LMR's, running between Birmingham and York though only one train in the day actually started from Birmingham. The majority of trains began at Bristol with one through from Cardiff and one from Worcester. The Bristol trains included the overnight Mails which had in their formation the well-known T.P.O. vehicles. The northern destination of most of the through trains was Newcastle. The other source of through trains was the residue of expresses which ran via Sheffield Vic-

There was nothing unusual in the sight of a dirty V2 on an up train in the morning and this is another instance of my not bothering to photograph although my friend Peter Tait again produced a rather pleasing picture. The train, M291, was the Filey Holiday Camp - King's Norton which passed at 11.44 on 3//8/57. The locomotive, 60848 of Gateshead (52A) shed, was a most unusual choice for this train although the train may have been a duplicate since B1 4-6-0 No. 61053 had gone by a few minutes earlier in more or less the same path. *(Peter Tait)*

| Table 1 | S & K Joint. | Summer Saturdays 1954 |
Down	Up	Train
	00/36	Newcastle - Bournemouth
01/20		Bristol - York
01/35		Bristol - Newcastle
04/30		Swindon - York
08.02		Sheffield - York (Slow)
	08.06	York - Sheffield (Midland) Slow
08.11		Sheffield (Vic) - Bridlington
08.48		Sheffield (Midland) - Scarborough (Central)
09.08		Sheffield (Victoria) - York
09.20		Sheffield (Victoria) - Bridlington
	09.51	Newcastle - Paignton
10.04		Chesterfield (Midland) - Bridlington/Filey/Scarborough
	10.12	Sunderland - Bristol
10.15		Sheffield (Victoria) - Scarborough (L.Rd)
10.20		Derby - Scarborough (Central)
10.32		Sheffield (Midland) - Pontefract (Slow)
	10.36	Newcastle - Cardiff
10.47		Birmingham - Newcastle
	10.54	Newcastle - Bournemouth
11.10		Leicester (L.Rd) - Scarborough (Central)
11.15		Silkstone - Scarborough (L.Rd)
	11.15	Scarborough (L.Rd) - Leicester (L.Rd)
11.20		Sheffield (Vic) - Bridlington/Filey HC
	11.25	Filey HC - Kings Norton
11.38		Gloucester (E) - Filey HC
11.46		Kings Norton - Scarborough (Central)
	11.50	Pontefract - Sheffield (Midland) Slow
	12.00	Filey HC - Sheffield (Vic)
12.02		Manchester (L.Rd) - Brid/Scarborough
12.15		Worcester - York
	12.24	Scarborough (L.Rd) - Sheffield (Vic)
	12.30	York - Birmingham/Bristol
	12.40	Scarborough (L.Rd) - Manchester (L.Rd)
12.50		Newcastle - Swansea
	13.10	Scarborough (Central) - Kings Norton
	13.20	Filey - Derby (Midland)
	13.34	Scarborough (L.Rd) - Sheffield (Midland)
13.34		Birmingham - Newcastle
	13.40	Bridlington - Sheffield (Vic)
13.42		Bristol - Newcastle
	13.45	York - Sheffield (Midland) Slow
	13.52	Scarborough (Central) - Derby
	14.10	Scarborough (L.Rd) - Leicester (Central)
14.30		Cardiff - Newcastle
	14.40	York - Birmingham
	14.54	Newcastle - Bristol
15.15		Bournemouth - Newcastle
15.40		Bristol - Newcastle
	15.45	Bridlington - Sheffield (Victoria)
15.53		Sheffield (Midland) - York Slow
16.24		Swansea - York
16.52		Paignton - Newcastle
	18.10	Newcastle - Birmingham
18.56		Bournemouth - Newcastle
19.12		Sheffield (Midland) - York (Slow)
	19.28	York - Sheffield (Midland) Slow
19.32		Newquay - Newcastle
19.39		Bristol - York
	21.50	Hull - Pontefract (Mail)
	22.09	Newcastle - Bristol (Mail)
22.43		Newquay - York
	22.58	York - Swindon (Bristol). Mail

Notes: 1. Oblique sign indicates approximate passing times of non-stop trains

2. Starlight Specials not included.

Throughout the decade of the 1950s I never saw a single BR Britannia on the S&K line - they were very rare. No. 70013 OLIVER CROMWELL (32A:Norwich) was the first I ever observed when it very unexpectedly turned up on the Newcastle - Bournemouth through train on 23 July 1960, shown here entering Baghill from the north. It was most unusual to see any locomotive from an East Anglian shed except for March (31B) which occasionally seemed to provide a V2 for the Cardiff or Bournemouth train. By the time of this photograph the branch to the L&Y had been relaid for the new Pontefract - Leeds (Central) service which ran via the Methley Joint Line. Another more unfortunate change, visually, was the appearance of the heavy cabling suspended from the telegraph poles, which rather spoilt the photography in an otherwise photogenic location.

toria and the G.C. Line; these included the Newcastle/York - Bournemouth, Newcastle/York - Swansea together with those which ran between Swindon and York (also including mails). The ordinary service was completed by odd stopping trains between Sheffield (Midland) and York and Sheffield (Victoria) and York.

For a while there were a few Sheffield (Mid) - Pontefract local services which turned round at Pontefract and returned to Sheffield, supplying an all-stations service and connections from smaller places en route into following main line trains at Baghill. The 1954 table shows the last vestige of this practice in the 9-40 a.m. (S.O.) stopper which arrived at 10.32 a.m. and started back to Sheffield at 11-50 a.m. From 1955 this train began to work through to York in its own right and eased crowding on the following Birmingham - Newcastle train. In a similar kind of way there were at one time a few Hull - Pontefract locals which ran via Selby and terminated at Baghill and these also fed into southbound main line services; one of these clung on to existence well after the others had

This picture relates directly to BRILL Summer Special No. 1, where on page 55, BR Class 9F No. 92058 is shown on the turntable at Scarborough before leaving with the 12.15 to King's Norton. It is seen here, later in the same day, passing Pontefract on its way south. (23/7/60).

1959 saw the introduction of LMS Patriots to the line (apart from No. 45509 which had been at Derby for some years but was an infrequent performer on the S&K), having been displaced by the introduction of diesels on the LNW main line. 45504, 45506 and 45519 were surprisingly allocated to Bristol from which shed they took their place on the Bristol - Newcastle trains and I took many pictures of them in Pontefract. This picture shows No. 45506 ROYAL PIONEER CORPS leaving the station on the 10.43 to Newcastle (8.05 a.m. ex-Birmingham). The station junction signal box was derelict by this time with control of the simplified junction having passed to Pontefract South signal box, at the other end of the station. (June 1960)

Table 2 Down	Up	Train	Loco	Class	Shed	SUMMER SATURDAY 1953 Load
	09.00	Light Engine	61152	B1 4-6-0	39B (Sheffield Darnall)	
09.22		Sheffield - York	60975	V2 2-6-2	50A (York)	9
09.30		Troop special	44809	5MT 4-6-0	17A (Derby)	10
09.40		Special	44962	5MT 4-6-0	21A (Saltley)	10
09.50		Chesterfield - Bridlington	42857	5MT 2-6-0	21A (Saltley)	13
	09.53	Newcastle - Paignton	60868	V2 2-6-2	52A (Gateshead)	8
10.10		Derby - Scarborough	43859	4F 0-6-0	17A (Derby)	11
10.23		Empty Stock	42774	5MT 2-6-0	14A (Cricklewood)	10
10.30		Sheffield (Vic) - Scarborough	61914	K3 2-6-0	39A (Gorton)	10
10.35		Sheffield(Midland) - Pontefract		Compound	18C (Hasland)	4
	10.40	Newcastle - Cardiff	60806	V2 2-6-2	52B (Heaton)	11
11.03		Silkestone - Scarborough	64362	J11 0-6-0	36D (Barnsley)	8
	11.04	Newcastle - Bournemouth	61338	B1 4-6-0	50A (York)	11
11.15		Birmingham - Newcastle	45682	5XP 4-6-0	22A (Bristol)	11
11.20		Sheffield (Vic) - Filey HC	61869	K3 2-6-0	53A (Dairycoates)	6
	11.20	Scarborough - Leicester (MR)	61438	B16 4-6-0	50A (York)	11
	11.24	Additional	61434	B16 4-6-0	50A (York)	10
11.25		Leicester (MR) - Scarborough	44963	5MT 4-6-0	19B (Millhouses)	10
	11.30	Filey HC - Kings Norton	61414	B16 4-6-0	50B (Neville Hill)	12
11.35		Gloucester - Filey HC	60914	V2 2-6-2	34A (Kings Cross)	10
	11.40	Additional	61464	B16 4-6-0	50A (York)	9
11.43		Kings Norton - Scarborough	45407	5MT 4-6-0	19A (Sheffield)	9
	11.45	Pontefract - Sheffield		Compound	18C (Hasland)	4
12.03		Manchester (L.Rd) - Filey HC	61166	B1 4-6-0	36B (Mexborough)	9
	12.08	Filey HC - Sheffield (Vic)	60843	V2 2-6-2	50A (York)	8
12.14		Kings Norton - Scarborough	44542	4F 0-6-0	21A (Saltley)	9
	12.15	Scarborough - Sheffield (Vic)	61457	B16 4-6-0	50A (York)	8
12.20		Worcester - York	44811	5MT 4-6-0	21B (Bourneville)	11
	12.30	York - Bristol	44754	5MT 4-6-0	20A (Holbeck)	10
12.40		Scarborough - Manchester (L.Rd)	61018	B1 4-6-0	51B (Newport)	8
	12.50	Newcastle - Swansea	60820	V2 2-6-2	38B (Annesley)	11

4 hours : 31 locomotives : 10 different classes

ceased, but its main function was to bring mails to Pontefract to connect with the southbound T.P.O. In fact, Baghill station was quite busy with mail traffic in the late evening.

On the whole, local traffic was quite sparse but some of the trains were, at times, very substantial, particularly the 8-6 a.m. to Sheffield, which often loaded to eleven vehicles and in summer ran through to Bristol, though it still carried Class B headcode.

Holiday times and summer Saturdays in particular saw many additional trains and various reliefs to the main expresses. One interesting service not included in the public timetable which ran via the S&K joint line were the "Starlight Specials" which ran each day between Marylebone and Edinburgh and passed through Pontefract in the early hours of the morning, but I never saw anything of them.

Turning now to the holiday trains in a little more detail; these were of two main types: long-distance trains to the south west resorts of Paignton, Penzance and Newquay etc., some of which ran overnight, and a large number of trains from Sheffield and the Midlands to the Yorkshire coast *(cont. page 19)*

This picture has been published before but, perhaps, deserves another airing because of its relative rarity; there are probably not many pictures of Crosti 9Fs working passenger trains. The 2-10-0s were commonplace on S&K passenger duties in the summer but on this occasion - August 3, 1957 - 92024 (15A) was turned out for the Leicester (L.Rd.) to Scarborough train and this was unusual. Looking back to those days it is quite astonishing that I appear to have made no effort to photograph the locomotive on its return in the afternoon, when there might have been a decent chance of a smoke effect as it came up the gradient through Pontefract; I can only assume that I was otherwise engaged, but I wish I had made the effort! The presence of a Wellingborough engine on an S&K summer Saturday working can be explained by the fact that there was a regular Wellingborough - York goods working which was diagrammed for a 15A 2-10-0 (usually a non-Crosti type). The fact that the engine sat spare at York over the weekend made it an ideal candidate for use in the intervening period.

The 1.20 p.m. to Bristol (12.48 ex-York) rolling into the platform from the north on a sunny day in July 1960, when I was to be a passenger for the short ten minute journey to Moorthorpe. Although it was a long distance train it also served as an S&K stopper for passengers making local journeys. In the background is the 1.24 p.m. service to Leeds (Central) standing in the north bay platform. The subway railings are seen at the right of the picture. Midland-based Jubilees were common on the S&K as opposed to those from the former L&Y, so 45702 CO-LOSSUS (26A: Newton Heath) was quite rare here.

The last southbound holiday train of the day returning from the Yorkshire coast was the 2.30 p.m. Scarborough (Central) - Sheffield (Midland) which arrived in Pontefract at 3.56 p.m. and left at 4.00 p.m.; from 1961 it ran through to Bristol. The train is shown here entering the station on 4/7/59 behind BR Standard Class 5 No. 73171, the last member in the class list. The photograph was taken from the raised loading platform on the down side of the line.

The 1.45 p.m. slow for Sheffield (Mid) getting into its stride a few hundred yards south of the station, hauled by a 2MT Mogul. Millhouses shed had two of these Ivatts - the pioneer No. 46400 and No. 46494 - which frequently performed on this train when not working their normal Sheffield - Chinley duties. The latter is shown here with ten coaches behind the tender, which was considerably greater than the average load normally dealt with by these locomotives. On occasions the BR version of the class (78000) also appeared on this job. *(Peter Tait)*

In the mid 1950s Selby shed received a number of Ivatt Class 4 2-6-0s which worked from that shed on both freight and passenger trains and in particular replaced the D20s on the Hull - Pontefract mail. They also found occasional work on Saturday-only jobs on turns normally powered by B16 4-6-0s. This picture, taken on 6th July 1957, shows 43097 in charge of the Scarborough - Leicester Central train passing under the Swanhill Lane road bridge, which was virtually identical to the rail bridge over the A645 road, on the branch to the L&Y line.

This location is roughly the southern extremity of the town; beyond the train the line is more or less level and begins its series of curves to bring the level down to that of the Plain of York at Ferrybridge, about three miles away. On this particular day (25/7/59) 4F 0-6-0 No. 44585 leans to the first of these curves with a train that my notes at the time describe as a Nottingham - Newcastle relief, which - if my record is correct - suggests that the LM were running rather short of both engines and stock.

The Pontefract loop line was an S&K branch which left Baghill just north of the station and ran to Pontefract East Junction on the L&Y line by means of a long, one-sided horseshoe curve about three-quarters of a mile in length. During the 1950s it was not much used but when it was, it was usually for special local excursions. The line was singled but not relaid late in 1956 and was at its lowest ebb in 1959 before being relaid, still as single track, for the introduction of the new Pontefract (Baghill) - Leeds (Central) service over the Methley Joint Line. This picture show a Kippax - Cleethorpes excursion on in June 1960 crossing to the main line just before Baghill Station. Class B1 No. 61035 PRONGHORN was a Neville Hill locomotive and a regular performer on such trips.

This 10/6/61 picture shows a Black 5-hauled special for Pontefract Races (probably from Sheffield or Chesterfield) taking the curve round to the L&Y line and just pulling away from the main York line which runs off to the left. Pontefract (Tanshelf) was the station nearest to the race course and this train would pass through Baghill, Monkhill and Tanshelf stations in order to gain its destination; these specials were some of the few trains that would pass through all three Pontefract stations. Most loop line trains came off the Methley branch at Monkhill.

At times ex-LNER Pacifics were rostered for S&K line trains, but in the main they were unpredictable and turned up on a number of different duties. A2 pacific 60524 HERRINGBONE was perhaps the most common one, being shedded at York for many years. On 30/8/58 (my note at the time says) I photographed the locomotive leaving Baghill at 9.49 on the Newcastle - Paignton train which avoided Sheffield by taking the "Old Road" from Rotherham to Derby; this train was not booked to stop at Chesterfield so it is possible that the engine worked through to Derby where it was due at 11.31. A note I made at the time records that No. 60524 was heading a Bristol - Newcastle on return and it appears to be the Saturdays only train that left Derby at 12 noon, but this implies too tight a turn-round at Derby. I can't explain this situation unless the locomotive came off the train at Rotherham and worked light into Sheffield to work the Newcastle train from there.

Although freight trains on Saturday mornings in summer were most unusual since there were no suitable paths for them, no photographic account of the S&K would be complete without a shot of an austerity . On 20/6/59 the summer timetable was not yet in full swing and thus room could be found for WD 2-8-0 90663 which scurries through, valves lifting, with a lightweight ballast train.

It is easy to run away with the idea that all those Saturdays in the 1950s were brilliantly sunny, for we normally only photographed in those conditions. On 31/8/57 I (rather unusually) chose to photograph in very wet conditions in the cutting to the south of the station, sheltering between times under the Carleton Road bridge. We were quite lucky in finding two Pacifics on up trains at roughly the same time; A1 60153 FLAMBOYANT is approaching the camera on the Sunderland - Bristol service while A3 60060 THE TETRARCH had gone through about ten minutes earlier with with the Newcastle - Paignton working. Both were relative strangers to the S&K, the former being one of York's roller-bearing Pacifics, more usually employed on Kings Cross services.

1960 saw the introduction of LMS Royal Scots to the S&K, following the transfer of several to Sheffield (Millhouses) from the LNWR, having been ousted by the first English Electric Type 4s, although back in 1949 we used to see 46120 when it regularly worked down to York from Derby for a period. No. 46131 THE ROYAL WARWICKSHIRE REGIMENT, seen here on a Nottingham - Newcastle relief train to the 8.05 a.m. Birmingham - Newcastle express, was evidently a rather poor performer and not generally up to the standard of the the rest of the class, by all accounts. The train is getting into its stride as it leaves the station for York and Newcastle. (6/8/

My memory of this rather unusual double-header is very hazy; Peter Tait's notebook shows it as the Newcastle - Cardiff through train leaving Pontefract on 2/8/58 and running about a quarter of an hour late. I am visible (near the fifth coach of the train) photographing also, but I have no note of it. I was under the impression for many years that it was a train bound for the G C Section and therefore might have been a relief for the following Bournemouth, which was hauled by Class V2 No. 60855, but it can't be both. It may be that a reader can shed some light on this working. The locomotives are Class K3 No. 61841 (Woodford) and Class 9F No. 92169 (Doncaster). *(Peter Tait)*

Pontefract (Baghill) was not an easy station to photograph as it was located on a curve and had staggered platforms. This view is from the up main platform looking south, showing the main building. The station had five platforms and was in effect a small two-platform terminus at the end of the branch from Pontefract (Monkhill, L&Y) together with up and down main platforms and a bay platform at the south end. The main line was crossed by means of a subway (visible here on the left of the picture) rather than to the more usual footbridge.

| Table 3 | | | SATURDAY 29 June 1957 | | | |
Down	Up	Train		Loco	Class	Shed
08.00		Sheffield - York Slow			5XP 4-6-0	
	08.06	York - Bristol			5MT 4-6-0	
08.17		Sheffield (Vic) - Bridlington		61166	B1 4-6-0	36B (Mexborough)
08.28		Light engine		63382	Q6 0-8-0	50C (Selby)
08.50		Sheffield (Midland) - Filey		41199	4P 4-4-0	19B (Millhouses)
09.09		Sheffield (Victoria) - York		62666	D11 4-4-0	41A (Darnall)
09.19		Private excursion		45667	5XP 4-6-0	16A (Nottingham)
09.40		Sheffield (Victoria) - Bridlington		61448	B16 4-6-0	50A (York)
	09.53	Newcastle - Paignton		60962	V2 2-6-2	52B (Heaton)
10.00		Chesterfield - Filey		45264	5MT 4-6-0	17B (Burton)
	10.14	Sunderland - Bristol		60132	A1 4-6-2	52A (Gateshead)
10.14		Additional		45114	5MT 4-6-0	3A (Bescot)
10.22		Derby - Scarborough		42872	5MT 2-6-0	17A (Derby)
10.33		Sheffield (Vic) - Scarborough		61867	K3 2-6-0	36B (Mexborough)
	10.35	Newcastle - Cardiff		73164	BR5 4-6-0	50A (York)
10.43		Sheffield - York (Slow)		46400	2MT 2-6-0	19B (Millhouses)
10.53		Birmingham - Newcastle		45577	5XP 4-6-0	22A (Bristol)
	10.55	Newcastle - Bournemouth		60954	V2 2-6-2	50A (York)
	11.14	Scarborough - Leicester (L.Rd)		61445	B16 4-6-0	50E (Scarborough)
11.19		Leicester (L.Rd) - Scarborough		45607	5XP 4-6-0	19B (Millhouses)
11.29		Sheffield (Vic) - Bridlington		61423	B16 4-6-0	50A (York)
	11.32	Filey HC - Kings Norton		41199	4P 4-4-0	19B (Millhouses)
11.37		Additional		45429	5MT 4-6-0	3E (Monument Lane)
11.45		Kings Norton - Scarborough		45040	5MT 4-6-0	21A (Saltley)
	12.03	Filey HC - Sheffield (Vic)		61454	B16 4-6-0	50A (York)
12.14		Worcester - York		44964	5MT 4-6-0	21A (Saltley)
	12.21	Additional		60974	V2 2-6-2	50A (York)
12.23		Manchester (L.Rd) - Filey		61114	B1 4-6-0	36A (Doncaster)
	12.29	York - Sheffield (Mid) Slow		61115	B1 4-6-0	50A (York)

29 locomotives : 13 different classes

resorts of Bridlington, Filey, Filey Holiday Camp and Scarborough. This latter group could be divided into two sub-groups: those coming off the Midland lines and those from the former G.C. lines, though not all travelled via Sheffield. In the case of the city of Sheffield itself, trains ran to the Yorkshire coast from both Midland and Victoria stations. Some trains came from the LMR: those from Leicester (London Road), Gloucester and King's Norton actually by-passed Sheffield and ran via the "Old Road" from Chesterfield to Rotherham and thence to the S&K, though not making any stops at any S&K stations. In similar fashion some trains to the G.C. south of Sheffield Victoria by-passed the city by using the Darnall curve, as with the "Starlight Specials" - the Scarborough to Leicester (Central) train was one such. There was also one other G.C. route which came into passenger use on summer Saturdays and this was the Wath Curve which enabled trains to come off the G.C. Manchester line on to the S&K Jt. without passing through Sheffield Victoria. The Silkstone - Scarborough and Manchester (London Road) - Scarborough trains used this route and provided such towns as

The return working of the 10.36 ex Sheffield slow left York at 1.00 p.m. and formed the 1.45 stopping service from Baghill to Sheffield (Midland); on this occasion motive power was provided by Millhouses Jubilee 45725 REPULSE. The train is made up of at least ten coaches and is shown pulling away from the south end of the station. The south-facing bay is clearly visible alongside the main platform. The stock in the background is that of a race special which is being stabled for the afternoon by No. 45428, one of the Class 5s now preserved. *(Peter Tait 7/6/58)*

Barnsley and Penistone with through services to the east coast.

In the northbound direction trains reached the Yorkshire coast by one of two routes: either directly to York and thence to Scarborough or via Gascoigne Wood and Selby and thence to Bridlington via Driffield. In this latter connection, the Mildford Junction, Gascoigne Wood area became a locomotive changing point for many trains from the south and west. This brief outline gives some idea of the summer Saturday service as a whole but more detail can be gleaned from Table 1.

The joint nature of the S&K line was, of course, most obviously apparent in the locomotive and coaching stock to be seen day by day. In the early days of my enthusiasm, at the very beginning of the BR era in the late 1940s, while the company colours were still to be seen, we would observe every day, full rakes of coaches from all the "Big Four" companies at one time or another, the Newcastle - Swansea and the Newcastle - Bournemouth services providing the GWR and SR representatives. Long-distance trains changed locomotives at either York or Sheffield (or both) which meant that we were able to observe LMS locomotives running through from Bristol to York and LNER locomotives running through from Newcastle to Sheffield, though it was quite common for trains from Newcastle to change engines at

Table 4			SATURDAY 3 August 1957		
Down	Up	Train	Loco	Class	Shed
09.10		Sheffield (Vic) - York	61096	B1 4-6-0	31A (Cambridge)
	09.10	Additional	44666	5MT 4-6-0	21A (Saltley)
09.20		Light engine	63450	Q6 0-8-0	50C (Selby)
09.35		Sheffield (Vic) - Bridlington	61426	B16 4-6-0	50A (York)
	09.49	Newcastle - Paignton	60941	V2 2-6-2	50A (York)
09.56		Chesterfield - Filey	44856	5MT 4-6-0	17A (Derby)
	10.18	Sunderland - Bristol	60807	V2 2-6-2	52A (Gateshead)
10.26		Derby - Scarborough	42824	5MT 2-6-0	17B (Burton)
10.39		Sheffield (Vic) - Scarborough	61424	B16 4-6-0	50A (York)
	10.45	Newcastle - Cardiff	61929	K3 2-6-0	31B (March)
10.48		Sheffield (Mid) - York (Slow)	46494	2MT 2-6-0	19B (Millhouses)
	10.54	Relief	48508	8F 2-8-0	19C (Canklow)
10.55		Nottingham - Newcastle (Relief)	45610	5XP 4-6-0	17A (Derby)
11.01		Relief	42764	5MT 2-6-0	Kettering
	11.01	Newcastle - Bournemouth	61291	B1 4-6-0	51A (Darlington)
11.10		Birmingham - Newcastle	45699	5XP 4-6-0	22A (Bristol)
11.16		Leicester (L.Rd) - Scarborough	92024	9F(c) 2-10-0	15A (Wellingborough)
	11.17	Scarborough - Leicester (L.Rd)	61445	B16 4-6-0	50E (Scarborough)
	11.22	Filey HC - Kings Norton	61053	B1 4-6-0	50A (York)
11.23		Sheffield (Vic) - Filey	61466	B16 4-6-0	50A (York)
	11.44	Filey - Kings Norton (Additonal)	60848	V2 2-6-2	52A (Gateshead)
11.45		Kings Norton - Scarborough	42790	5MT 2-6-0	21A (Saltley)
12.04		Manchester (L>Rd) - Filey	61036	B1 4-6-0	36A (Doncaster)
	12.04	Filey HC - Sheffield (Vic)	73169	BR5 4-6-0	50A (York)
12.16		Worcester - York	45269	5MT 4-6-0	21A (Saltley)
12.26		Light engines	90550/668	WD 2-8-0	36A (D'ter)/36B (Mexborough)
	12.35	Additional	61437	B16 4-6-0	50A (York)
	12.40	Scarborough - Manchester (L.Rd)	73168	BR5 4-6-0	50A (York)
	12.50	York - Sheffield (Slow)	42758	5MT 2-6-0	21A (Saltley)
	13.02	Newcastle - Swansea	61096	B1 4-6-0	31A (Cambridge)
	13.11	York - Bristol	44944	5MT 4-6-0	19C (Canclow)

4 hours : 32 locomotives : 14 different classes

Note rare use on passenger work of Crosti-boilered 2-10-0 92024 and Stanier 8F 48508. Also two GE locomotives seen far from their normal sphere of operations.

The 2.15 p.m. Bristol - York train, which stopped at Pontefract at varying times over the years around 7.25 p.m., was nicely photographable from the north western side of the line on summer evenings whilst being worked by Jubilee 4-6-0 45664 NELSON. This June 1960 view shows the train emerging from the cutting to the south of the station and passing the South Box's outer home signal which, at this time, was still of the N.E. wooden slotted-arm type. Over the years Bristol Jubilees predominated on this train, although at this particular period Millhouses locomotives, very often a Scot, were regular performers.

Private excursions carrying large headboards were the subject of a recent FOURUM article in BRILL, and many of these came over the S&K to the Yorkshire coast, from such places as Sheffield, Derby, Nottingham and Leicester. I managed quite a few photographs of them but they were not usually seen on Saturdays, in my experience. On the occasion of the June 29th observations this private excursion from Sandiacre came through Baghill at 9.19 a.m. behind a nicely cleaned up Jubilee No. 45667 JELLICOE of Nottingham Shed. At that time the camera I was using had a top shutter speed of 1/200 sec. and a little judicious panning was necessary when trying to photograph a non-stop passenger train and this is probably evident from the slight blur of the background.

The grazing cattle on the right of the picture seem hardly to be disturbed by the passing of the up Bournemouth train on 14/6/58, even though Class B16/3 No. 61448 has eleven coaches in tow and is lifting its train up the incline out of Baghill Station and making no small noise. 61448 was one of the B16s rebuilt by Thompson in 1944, a result of which was to reduce the severe appearance of the NER's original design. The day was hot and rather misty and there is no trace of either smoke or steam from the locomotive chimney. Needless to say, the field where the cattle were grazing is now covered with housing. *(Peter Tait)*

ABOVE : Although I do not recognize the reporting number, this train appears to be the late running 8.27 a.m. Derby - Scarborough (Central), shown crossing Grovetown bridge near the goods yard to the south of the station; this train had no stops on the S&K Jt. line. The locomotive is Hughes/Fowler Class 5F 2-6-0 No. 42822, fitted with Reidinger rotary valve gear, one of the quintet based at Burton at this time. In conversation recently I was given to understand that Burton shed frowned on the use of these locomotives on passenger work, but they were certainly much in evidence on such trains as these and I photographed all except No. 42825 on them. On this particular date, 2/8/58, No. 42824 had also gone through, on a similar train, only half an hour earlier. *(Peter Tait)*

BELOW : This side-on view from the middle of the field to the north east of the station shows the twelve coach Newcastle - Bournemouth train slowing for the Pontefract stop, behind B1 No. 61291 (51A) on 3/8/57. Darlington engines were not all that common on the S&K and the locomotive is showing signs of smokebox scorching - it may be that the engine was a hasty replacement for a failed V2 as the train was nearly a quarter of an hour late at this point.

This picture shows something of the lie of the land in Pontefract. The hill in the right background is called Bag Hill (or Baghill) and gave its name to the station, while the wooded hill in the centre background is the site of the castle ruins, one of those Cromwell "knocked about a bit". During the sieges of Pontefract Castle in the 1640s, when it was one of the most impregnable fortresses in the north of England, it was bombarded from Baghill by Cromwell's forces and one of the siege works was actually located on the rising face of the hill, behind the houses on the right. The S&K line passed through the town in a sweeping S-bend to join the North Eastern line at Ferrybridge, which is in the centre background about two miles beyond the town. This picture, taken on 20/6/59, shows the Scarborough (Londesborough Road) - Leicester (Central) train passing through Pontefract behind B16/1 No. 61422 and was one that went to the GC Section without going into Sheffield (Victoria). (This photograph was taken on the same day as the workings referred to in the Bridlington article in BRILL Summer Special No. 1).

23

The 8.36 a.m. Sheffield (Victoria) - Bridlington train made one stop on the S&K at Moorthorpe, but passed through Pontefract non-stop at about 9.30 a.m. This view of 19/7/58, from the end of the up main platform, shows the train about to pass through behind Class B16/1 No. 61416. This was one of the class which remained pretty well unaltered - others were rebuilt by Gresley and Thompson - and nothing, perhaps, personifies the NER quite so much as the cab - completely utilitarian with no concessions to style whatever. The wooden shed on the right was known as the Malt Shed and the main goods warehouse is dimly discernible behind the first coach. Pontefract South signal box is in the distance, just to the left of the gas lamp.

York and again at Sheffield.

A glance at Tables 2, 3 and 4 gives quite a good idea of locomotive variety on summer Saturdays and it is unnecessary to repeat that here; the photographic captions give more detail in terms of comment about individual locomotive classes and the trains themselves.

Locomotive variety to be seen in the late 1940s was, of course, much greater and some of the numerically small classes which survived the war for a few years were much in evidence on summer Saturdays. Particular favourites of mine were the GC/LNER B7s, common on trains from Sheffield Victoria, together with a few of the last remaining GN/LNER C1s which appeared from time to time on Bridlington trains, though it could not be claimed that they were common. I well remember one of the last C1s running into Baghill about 3-15 or so on a return working to Sheffield (Victoria) and being unable to restart its train until it had set back two or three times and only then, with apparently great effort, did it manage to get its train on the move. The southbound start out of Baghill was not very easy; the station is on a curve and the gradient is about 1 in 150, so if the rails were at all greasy, locomotives were apt to slip. The most impressive departure I remember was made by Jubilee No. 5610 GOLD COAST, which lifted the afternoon Bristol train (loaded to fourteen coaches) out of the station in pouring rain without trace of a slip.

On the Midland side the 4-4-0 classes 2P, 3P and 4P were much more common (as would be expected) than at the time of these observations, but, up to 1959, the Compounds were still making their sporadic appearances and the last one I photographed was No. 40907 in May 1959.

One noticeable feature of locomotive working on the S&K Jt. was the almost total absence of tank locomotives - there was no really suitable work for them, apart from the Sheffield Pontefract locals which sometimes produced a Millhouses 2-6-2T. During the winter timetable of 1949 there was a morning Hull - Pontefract train (and return) which made main line connections at Baghill and which produced regularly one of the Hull L1 2-6-4Ts (then in apple green) and it was a great pity that it was taken off for the summer timetable, when its usefulness would have been much enhanced. Otherwise, apart from tank locomotives making their way to Gorton or Darlington Works, they were virtually unknown. Even the evening Hull - Pontefract mail train was dominated by tender locomotives, from Selby shed: in the early 1950s D20s monopolized the train, though I did see the odd G5 or A8 on it, but after the disappearance of the D20s it became the preserve of the LMR Ivatt Class 4MT Moguls which by now were infiltrating the N.E. Region.

March 1958 saw the introduction of Diesel Multiple Units on the L&Y side of town but it wasn't until 1959 that a number of local services on the S&K line became dieselized; even so, main line services remained in the hands of steam for the most part until late in 1961, though the bad winter of 1961-62 saw a resurgence of steam power for a while. After 1962 my photographic activities much diminished on my own patch and it is a matter of great regret that I did not cover the next five years or so, when there were many interesting workings, especially when steam power substituted for failed diesels and when more glamorous locomotive types, having been displaced from passenger duties, were to be seen on freight duties.

Although the S&K line still carries a decent amount of freight traffic it is not now part of the North East - South West trunk route and Baghill Station is now a sad sight; somehow or other British Rail have contived to "manage" it almost out of existence, there remaining only a derisory Sheffield - Pontefract - York service that hardly anyone can use. However, it is not the intention of this article to muse over the present scene, but to try to give a glimpse of the way things were in the 1950s when at busy times, both booking office windows at Baghill Station were open for business and queues of holiday makers stretched out through the booking hall and on to the road outside.

I would like to acknowledge here the help given to me by my friend Peter Tait, with whom I spent a number of those Saturday mornings by the lineside, in allowing me to use some of his pictures to supplement my own. In addition I would very much like to hear from anyone who has relevant information and particularly photographs of the S&K line (and the Pontefract area in general) in the period before I got going in the middle 1950s.

All photographs by the author unless stated otherwise.

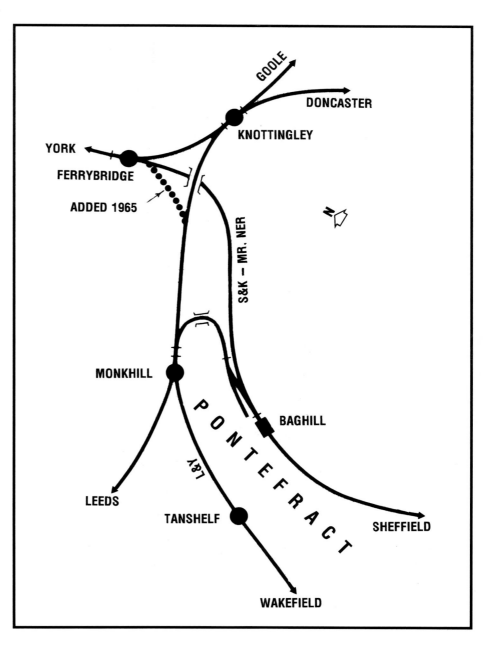

Fourum *Long to rain over us......*

Just to remind readers that this BRILL volume ostensibly marks the British summer, these two pages recall the usual weather to found in those good old black and white summers of yore - rosy tinted remembrances of never ending August sunshine aside. Rain seemed to have dogged Leslie Sandler in his early 'sixties mission to record steam but he took a chance with this shot of Schools 4-4-0 30930 RADLEY, at Guildford on the 10.50am Wolverhampton - Ramsgate train, on a glorious (?) 6th August 1962.

Grim determination on the face... Ivatt 2-6-2 'Teddy-bear' 41233 bears a Bangor shedplate which should set this scene in North Wales. The rain is a useful piece of circumstantial evidence. I speak as one who spent several summers working in Snowdonia, and the steam hanging around is, to my jaundiced memory, indistinguishable from the low cloud frequently wreathing everything above about 50 feet. So just where is this? The first correct answer, accompanied by a decent "steam in the rain" photograph capable of starring in BRILL, will bring the reward of a year's subscription. Answers should also include a suitable conversation between the two crew members...

The West Country of course always promised the best of summers. In another of Leslie Sandler's lovely studies he captures that more familiar British experience - not the sun, so much as the aftermath of rain. If there truly is always sunshine after rain, then this bit of Great Westernry is it. 4574 at Launceston on the 7.10am ex-Plymouth, 23rd August 1962.

Bit of a cheat this one (it's March - illustrating how difficult it is to find decent pictures taken in the rain). Most people, of course, never bothered. Great Cumbrae rises out of the grey Firth of Clyde in the distance as hikers and other visitors make their way down rainswept Fairlie Pier, off the 9.27am relief Arran boat train from Glasgow on Good Friday, 24th March 1967. This was the last such working to be steam hauled and the crew of Corkerhill Black Five No.44699 clearly relished the occasion; the Scottish Region finished with steam traction five weeks later. Fairlie Pier station originally had twin wooden train sheds stretching a considerable way down the curved platform and the remains of these can be seen on the left. Ardrossan has since replaced Fairlie as the Arran terminal, somewhat unfortunately, as the former harbour can be difficult to make in certain weather conditions, resulting in time consuming diversions to Gourock. *Photograph W.A.C. Smith; caption notes from an original by Paul Anderson.*

As experienced by
PARSIFAL

How did we let them go...? With scant regard for the ban on steam south of Peterborough imposed in the summer of 1963, steam continued to reach Kings Cross until the end of that year, many of the incursions being caused by poor diesel availability. One such case occurred on 31 July 1963 when A1 4-6-2 60119 PATRICK STIRLING, seen here backing out of the terminus, arrived with the 09.25 'Norseman' from Newcastle. *Photograph Andrew Ockwell.*

DIESEL DAWN Trials and Tribulations on the

GREAT NORTHERN

Thirty years ago, as someone with a passion for railways and the East Coast in particular, I found myself in the favoured position of being able to monitor - and to some extent influence - engine movements on the East Coast main line and those of the Kings Cross Division in particular. Coupled with this was the ability - long before MAS signalling became a working reality - to be able to see, over a long distance, how individual trains on the GN section of the East Coast main line were running.

My attitude - and that of my immediate colleagues - towards diesels was one of optimistic curiosity. Only a few years ago railways and steam had been inextricably linked - the terms were synonymous - and the withdrawal of old friends could be likened to losing a close relative. On the other hand the promised advantages of the new order and the novelty in being able to operate at speeds which had hitherto been rare suggested that perhaps the time was ripe for a change. In addition we had been promised - no less - that the financial troubles which had

afflicted BR since the late 1950s would be swept away once the new heaven of dieselisation had become a fact. There was not, in my recollection, an automatic prejudice against the new order at its inception.

At the time in which this article concerns itself dieselisation of the Great Northern had just about been completed - the exception was a batch of BR 2-10-0s which continued to work the heavy coal traffic between New England and Colwick - and with it a new system of locomotive control of which I was a (minor) part.

The allocation of steam engines to diagrams and trains had traditionally been the responsibility of the Motive Power Depot, not unreasonably since much of a steam engine's day was spent on shed either being prepared or disposed and it would have been impossible for an outsider to have kept in meaningful touch with all that went on. Diesels, on the other hand, possessed a significant operational difference from steam since, in theory, they did not go on shed but remained in traffic either until either they broke

down or were required for maintenance. The general idea was that they remained in traffic for as long as there were trains to be worked. Thus it became necessary for an outside body to maintain a watching brief on engine movements and to see that their workings either went according to plan or made attempts to adjust things when the plan went awry.

Different parts of BR had different ways of performing the task but at Kings Cross two additional posts on each shift - a locomotive controller and an assistant - were created in the District control room, and I was fortunate to be amongst the first selected for one of the assistant posts. The requirements for being appointed were as vague as any on BR but the Operating Superintendent Bill Stirling (or, as we called him, sir) the man who ran the operational side of the GN single-handedly, appeared to favour people who had a deep interest in trains and a deeper one in the GN system of doing things. Thus the loco control assistants, and many others in the control, had a strong commitment to the

One would not suspect from the photograph, taken in August 1959, that Kings Cross still had an allocation of 40 0-6-2Ts and 17 L1 2-6-4Ts for its suburban traffic. One of the reasons for the retention of so much steam was the poor availability of the two classes illustrated. They were brand new and yet both, within a very short space of time, consigned themselves to oblivion. D6104, an 1100hp North British Type 2, was, with the rest of the class, transferred out of harms way to Eastfield, Glasgow, where they failed to replace the A4s on the Glasgow - Aberdeen workings, whilst the 1100hp Baby Deltics had to be withdrawn en masse for extensive rebuilding, not returning to traffic until 1964. In the background is a Cravens DMU getting ready to leave platform 11 with the 10.33 Kings Cross - Hertford North, whilst two BRCW Type 2s lurk in the darkness of the suburban station.

good running of the railway - our railway - and even though it was professional suicide to claim to be a railway enthusiast, most of us, in fact were. (The extra-mural interest in the job had numerous benefits. I was, at the time, one of the stop watch brigade and when on early turn, which finished at 15.00, would often take a trip to Grantham and back and was generally able to "negotiate' the particular engine I wanted to ride behind on the 16.20 or 17.05 departures from Kings Cross. Class 40s and 46s presented no especial problems but I never quite succeeded in getting a class 25 in the workings).

The GN main line diesel fleet fell into two categories. There were the purely local machines, which in those days included class 3ls, Class 25s, Class 20s, the Baby Deltics and

Paxman Type 1s; all were booked into diagrams by the running foremen at the depots involved; the engines and their workings being read over to the controller at the start of play, and the main line engines - Deltics, Class 47s, Cromptons and the Class 40s - were individually allocated to trains by the controller.

At the time there were quite a number of depots at the southern end of the Great Northern and although Kings Cross - top shed as it had been called - had closed with the end of steam, its running role as a stabling/refuelling point for engines between workings was taken over by Kings Cross loco whilst periodic examinations and certain repairs were performed at Clarence Yard depot, a mile south of Finsbury Park. The peripheral sheds (Hatfield, Hitchin, New Eng-

land and Grantham) survived as signing-on points for train crews and although they had no formal engine allocation, because diagrams started and finished at these points, many engines had to be stabled there, which had much the same effect as an allocation.

Suburban passenger engines - Class 3ls and 25s - were allocated to Hornsey whilst the Class 2Os and Paxman Type 1 engines took over the former N7 0-6-2T goods duties at Hatfield, which at that time still included the GN branch to Luton and Dunstable. The class 31 engines, which numerically were the mainstay of the internal workings, were not normally put on express passenger services other than the odd 'parliamentary' to Peterborough and one or two stock workings between Peterborough and

The first train to become regularly diesel-worked was the Master Cutler Pullman service between Sheffield (Victoria) and Kings Cross, a new working which inaugurated the use of class 40 locomotives on the GN. D207, which was later transferred to Stratford for the Liverpool St - Norwich services, arrives with the maiden run of the Cutler on 19 May 1958.

TABLE 1		DELTIC AVAILABILITY 30 MARCH - 5 APRIL 1966
ENGINE	DEPOT	AVAILABILITY
D9000	64B	DONCASTER REPAIRS MON & TUES
D9001	34G	DONCASTER WORKS THUR & FRI
D9002	52A	WORKED ALL WEEK
D9003	34G	FAILED FRIDAY. REPAIRS SATURDAY
D9004	64B	WORKED ALL WEEK
D9005	52A	WORKED ALL WEEK
D9006	64B	WORKED ALL WEEK
D9007	34G	FAILED LEEDS CENTRAL FRIDAY
D9008	52A	WORKED ALL WEEK
D9009	34G	FAILED AT YORK WEDNESDAY. TO DONCASTER WORKS FOR REPAIRS
D9010	64B	FAILED AT KINGS CROSS WEDNESDAY
D9011	52A	FAILED KINGS CROSS THURSDAY
D9012	34G	WORKED ALL WEEK
D9013	64B	FAILED NEAR KINGS CROSS
D9014	52A	GATESHEAD REPAIRS MONDAY-WEDNESDAY
D9015	34G	WORKED ALL WEEK
D9016	64B	FAILED KINGS CROSS THURSDAY
D9017	52A	WORKED ALL WEEK
D9018	34G	DONCASTER WORKS SATURDAY
D9019	52A	WORKED ALL WEEK
D9020	34G	WORKED ALL WEEK
D9021	64B	WORKED ALL WEEK

Doncaster. The exception was on summer Saturdays when one would be diagrammed to work the morning Skegness service from Kings Cross and this was probably the longest passenger working that any of the class involved themselves with. On the neighbouring Great Eastern matters were rather different and although the Type 3 and 4 locomotives were the diagrammed power for Kings Lynn and Norwich, it was quite common to see class 31s at work on the Kings Lynn duties.

In addition to its class 31s, Hitchin also had a number of workings for which it relied heavily on the Baby Deltics and many of them, although nominally allocated to Hornsey, turned round and were given basic maintenance in a new depot built on the down side to the north of the station.

Diesel multiple units tended to look after themselves - one heard very little from them - and were based at Western Sidings, close by the London side of Finsbury Park Station. The numbers of the units in each working were read over to us each morning by the foreman and that, generally, was all the contact we had with them. On one or two occasions we had to loco-haul a DMU working with a class 31 and a set of Gresley quads but such instances were very rare. The DMUs tended to monopolise the inner suburban service on both the main line and the new line (Hertford North) and in addition took on many of the lesser trains between London and points on the Cambridge branch. They also covered one main line service, the 10.25 'parly' to Peterborough, which made a sad contrast with the train when it had been steam worked, for the service had boasted a lengthy rake of corridor stock headed by a Pacific. Whilst touching the subject of the GN multiple units, two aspects of their operation stick in my mind. The first was the exceptionally smooth start the two-car sets used to make from platform 11 on the Hertford North trains which left at 3 and 33 minutes past the hour. There was none of the raucous acceleration that generally characterised DMU starts; the GN units simply glided with very little noise out of the station and into the tunnel. The second recollection was when the stock running in to form the 16.03 Kings Cross - Hertford one Friday managed to derail itself in the throat of the terminus and succeeded - in the prelude to the busiest part of the day - to paralyse matters in a way that even the Luftwaffe had failed to do.

Outside the London area the biggest depot was New England, near Peterborough, upon which were based a number of Class 47 workings, their main function to power the not infrequent coal trains to and from Ferme Park plus the power station services to Tempsford. In 1966 these workings were extended to include the workings to Colwick after the demise of the 2-10-0 'spaceships'. New England also had a regular service of trains to Whitemoor on the Great Eastern; most of these being in the hands of GE section Class 31 and 37 engines.

The three locomotive controllers - one for each shift - were all former footplatemen who had opted for a change of clothing at a relatively early age in the hope of better things. Two of the three had been main line firemen in the Newcastle link with their own A4 engines (MALLARD and QUICKSILVER respectively) whilst the third, sometimes regarded as a bit of an odd man out, had spent his time as a Hornsey 'loafer' working up and down the goods lines to and from New England on Austerity 2-8-0s. The character - and no other adjective suffices - that I found myself serving had been MALLARD's regular fireman for a number of years during the early 1950s and what a fount of tales he could come up with. Kings Cross was his church and the trains that the shed worked were his creed. He would speak in the most contemptuous terms of other depots and recounted (usually weekly) the day when he and his driver had worked a down main line duty as far as York where they disposed of the engine and lodged for the night. Whilst unhooking the engine in the station Jack Goddard (my mentor) scuttled off to the buffet and procured the largest crate of beer obtainable, lugged it onto the engine and, after settling the Pacific for the night, manhandled it into the mess room where the pair sat down and quaffed the lot, surrounded by thirsty looking York men - who were not even offered a smell of the empties.

The principal duty of the locomotive control was to allocate engines to down services from Kings Cross and several times in a turn of duty Liverpool Street HQ control - which in 1967 moved to York - would read over a list of up services and the engines working them and these would be allocated to down services, usually although not necessarily, according to the diagrammed working, by the Kings Cross

In the early days of their career, Brush-Sulzer Type 4 locomotives D1501 and D1503 pay a visit to Kings Cross top shed on 10 March 1963. How these engines have survived as front-rank locomotives for over thirty years, given their desperately poor availability during the 1960s is a minor mystery. At the time it was by no means unusual to find half the Clarence Yard allocation unavailable for work at any given time due to the high rate of failures and repairs. *Photograph Alec Swain.*

controller who would confirm them with Liverpool Street and then read them over to the running foreman at Kings Cross loco.

The role of the HQ control was to 'co-ordinate' the district controls with respect to foreign engines and now and again would attempt to test their authority on the divisions by refusing to

authorise the use of a particular engine. Since, however, they were rather remote from the operating function they were a rather ineffective group as Kings Cross demonstrated one morning when HQ refused to allow a Tinsley Class 47 - the only engine available because of an epidemic of failures - to work the 04.00 Kings Cross - Leeds.

King of the road. An unidentified Deltic emerges from Clarence Yard after periodic maintenance prior to running light to Kings Cross to work the 10.00 'Flying Scotsman' to Edinburgh. The engine is seen having its sandboxes replenished before leaving the yard confines, a practice which fell into disuse as it became clear that sand was not as necessary for diesel traction as it had been for steam. In contrast to other main line diesels, the Deltics were relatively trouble-free in service.

Pheonix risen from the ashes. When first delivered in 1959 the 1100hp Baby Deltics were of neither use not ornament to the Kings Cross operators amd spent most of the early 1960s rusting in sidings at Stratford. In 1964, however, they re-emerged, internally rebuilt and for the remainder of their existence performed usefully and reliably on the GN suburban workings. The headcode displayed by D5904, backing out of Kings Cross (Suburban) on 7 August 1964, is that of a stopping Cambridge service, the stock of which - note the use of corridor vehicles employed in some of the GN outer-suburban workings - stands in the adjacent platform. *Photograph Alec Swain.*

After some argument the Kings Cross controller gave in and accepted their dictum. At five past four the Kings Cross section controller tersely announced that the 04.00 was waiting engine and at ten past - still with no other engine available - the proscribed Tinsley engine was duly turned off the loco for the working. The resulting twenty minute delay and the row it caused later in the day ensured that HQ control in the years ahead maintained a low profile so far as decision making was concerned.

The assistant controllers performed a similar, if quieter, function to that of their masters in respect of Grantham (until the boundary was moved from Barkeston to Stoke) and New England and also maintained a graph upon which was recorded the activities of all Kings Cross allocated diesels Types 1 to 5.

This graph - a classic outpouring of some bureaucratic scheme, which never performed a useful purpose, occupied at least three quarters of the assistants' time. Lasting for a week at a time and to the scale of an inch per hour, engines were listed by class in numerical order and the assistant, perusing the controllers' booking out sheets and sets of diagrams, would laboriously graph whatever it was that each engine was doing at any given time. The original idea - at the time the control scheme was being conceived - was to provide the controller with instant information as to where any of his engines were at any given time.

The designers of the scheme, however, underestimated by a considerable extent the mental abilities of the controllers who, not long after taking duty, managed without difficulty to know quite instinctively where all their engines were and thus the graph, although meticulously maintained when new, never served any worthwhile purpose. (Early fears that the completed graph was later closely inspected by some clerical official located in some dark Fuhrerbunker in Great Northern House, bent on finding errors, were

The engines that kept us going....and those that didn't. Deltic D9020 NIMBUS, which has arrived south with the overnight 'Night Scotsman', stands alongside Brush-Sulzer D1501 outside Clarence Yard maintenance depot circa 1965. The class 47 locomotives - generally referred to as 'Hawker-Siddleys' by the GN - were, at the time of the photograph, rated at 2750hp. From 1966 they were derated to 2558hp.

TABLE 2	KINGS CROSS : MAINLINE DEPARTURES (1964)	
TIME	DESTINATION	LOCO.
01.00	NEWCASTLE /EDINBURGH	55
01.15	YORK	47
02.00	GRANTHAM	47
04.00	LEEDS CENTRAL	47
05.55	GRANTHAM	47
07.45	LEEDS/SHEFFIELD	55
08.00	EDINBURGH	55
08.20	DONCASTER	47
09.00	NEWCASTLE	55
09.20	LEEDS/BRADFORD	55
10.00	EDINBURGH/ABERDEEN	55
10.20	LEEDS/BRADFORD	55
10.25	PETERBOROUGH	DMU
11.00	ABERDEEN/GLASGOW	55
11.20	SHEFFIELD PULLMAN	47
12.00	LEEDS/GRASGOW PULLMAN	55
13.00	NEWCASTLE	47
13.20	LEEDS	47
14.00	EDINBURGH	55
14.20	YORK	40
15.00	NEWCASTLE	47
15.20	LEEDS/BRADFORD	47
16.05	CLEETHORPES	37
16.20	LEEDS/BRADFORD	47
16.43	PETERBOROUGH	47
17.00	NEWCASTLE PULLMAN	55
17.05	NEWCASTLE VIA SUNDERLAND	47
17.37	BRADFORD/HULL PULLMAN	55
18.05	NEWCASTLE	55
18.12	YORK	47
18.17	PETERBOROUGH	31
18.40	LEEDS/BRADFORD VIA LYR	46
18.50	CLEETHORPES	37
19.20	SHEFFIELD PULLMAN	47
19.24	PETERBOROUGH	31
19.30	ABERDEEN/FORT WILLIAM	55
20.20	EDINBURGH	55
22.15	ABERDEEN	55
22.30	EDINBURGH	55
23.20	EDINBURGH	40
23.35	EDINBURGH	55
23.55	NEWCASTLE	55

In transit. Standing at the north end of Hornsey MPD in 1960 are three classes of engine, all destined to be transferred away within the space of a few years. The English Electric Type 4 - the first main line diesel to work on the GN - disappeared to the Great Eastern in 1962 whilst D6126, an NB Type 2, was sent to Scotland and, after a very brief period of life north of the border, to the scrapheap. The English Electric Type 1s were a succesful class and remained on the system - principally at Hatfield - until the demise of GN freight traffic in 1966 after which they were transferred to Immingham.

the glare. The blue crayon - 'engine available for work' - was by a long margin the least-used item of equipment.

From my point of view the best of all the three turns of duty was the night shift which started at 22.00 and went on until eight the next morning. From an enthusiast's standpoint it was almost worth paying to be there since within the confines of one small room were echoes of every Great Northern activity. Not only was it possible to follow everything that was taking place but occasionally one made a contribu-

tion. One such occurred at about half-past seven one morning when Hornsey loco rang in to say that the engine booked light to New Barnet for the 08.24 passenger to Broad Street had failed and that nothing was available to take its place. In those days the notion of cancelling a train - even the rudest of locals - was unthinkable - but with the limited time available to find a substitute, matters were looking bleak until out of the blue two SR type 2s (Class 33s) appeared at Ferme Park to work forward an Uddingstone - Cliffe cement train that had been can-

Quietly reliable. Before being stripped of its freight traffic in 1966, Kings Cross possessed no fewer than 31 0-6-0 diesel shunters, most of which were the standard 350hp variety, concentrated in the Kings Cross/Ferme Park area. Hitchin's shunting requirements were usually taken care of by a couple of Gardner 204hp locomotives but in this instance D3128 of the larger variety draws an engineers train out of Hitchin permanent way yard onto the down main line on 1 May 1964. Standing at the down home signal and waiting for a road through the station is a BTH 800 Type 1, another class of engine not normally seen so far to the north. Their main employment lay with the refuse trains between Ashburton Grove and Ayot plus a number of ECS workings at Kings Cross. *Photograph Alec Swain.*

also found to be misplaced after a series of tests which shewed some of the Hatfield Class 20s working on the PLM between Gare de Lyon and Marseilles - D8020 flat batteries: Dijon - produced no comment whatsoever).

What the graph did do was to show in blinding colours the general state of the fleet. Engines that had failed and were undergoing repairs had a red line ruled against them whilst those undergoing major surgery were given a yellow line and all too often one stood back from the canvass to be assailed by a depressing mass of red and yellow, especially in the area of the graph concerned with the Class 47s. One comic used to keep a pair of sunglasses in his jacket and would don them as he passed in order to protect his eyes from

TABLE 3.		CLARENCE YARD CLASS 47 CYCLE (1965)		
DAY	ARR	POINT	DEP	TRAIN
1		HOLLOWAY	10.50	ECS
	14.41	DONCASTER	19.48	GOODS
	00.35	KINGS X GDS		
2		KINGS CROSS	02.00	PASSENGER
	04.00	GRANTHAM		ECS
		LINCOLN	07.10	EXPRESS
	09.50	KINGS CROSS	11.50	PARCELS
	14.40	DONCASTER	21.30	ECS
	04.40	BOUNDS GREEN		
3		KINGS CROSS	08.20	EXPRESS
	11.22	DONCASTER	13.47	EXPRESS
	16.54	KINGS CROSS		
		KINGS X GDS	19.55	GOODS
4	03.30	LEEDS CENTRAL	07.50	EXPRESS
	11.30	KINGS CROSS	16.20	EXPRESS
	20.08	LEEDS CENTRAL		LIGHT
5		DONCASTER	01.15	GOODS
	06.30	FERME PARK	09.25	EMPTIES
	13.53	NEW ENGLAND	21.15	ECS
	23.10	KINGS CROSS		
6		KINGS X GDS	00.37	GOODS
	02.50	PETERBOROUGH	07.22	PASSENGER
	09.22	KINGS CROSS	13.20	EXPRESS
	16.52	LEEDS CENTRAL	20.05	GOODS
	03.10	KINGS X GDS		
7		KINGS CROSS	09.04	PASSENGER
	10.26	CAMBRIDGE	11.08	PASSENGER
	12.34	KINGS CROSS	13.09	PASSENGER
	14.37	CAMBRIDGE	15.15	PASSENGER
	16.40	KINGS CROSS	19.34	PASSENGER
	21.55	PETERBOROUGH		
8		NEW ENGLAND	02.10	COAL
	06.24	FERME PARK		

A mighty Deltic rests whilst undergoing a major maintenance examination at Clarence Yard in March 1965. The buffers have been removed and the top doors opened to allow access to the brake exhausting mechanism. Note the buckeye coupling to the left of the fitters head. These were a legacy from the A4 Pacifics, the only steam engines to be so fitted, although those on the Deltics were not used in everyday operations.

celled by general circular about a week before. (The Southern at that time had no control system and everything operated to some sort of grand design irrespective of whether the traffic was on hand or not).

"Why not put the Hornsey men of the failure on the Southern engines, let the SR men act as loco conductors and send them down to Barnet for the 08.24?"/

Goddard looked at me and said that I was not always as stupid as I looked.

Half an hour later, camera in hand, I was on the first train down to Finsbury Park and travelled to Broad Street on what must have been the only occasion two SR Type 2s worked a passenger train into the NLR terminus. What was just as satisfying as the unusual event itself was the fact that the 08.24 was on time throughout.

At the beginning of the shift both Ferme Park and New England would have finished making up the night trains and the first hour or so would be occupied by the Peterborough section controller and the man in charge - The Deputy Chief Controller - discussing which loads should be taken by which trains to Ferme Park. All the section controllers would be engrossed with the stock reports from their yards to determine which goods trains they could dispense with and divert or whether additional engines would be needed for special trains.

In the London area the night trains to Aberdeen (22.15), Edinburgh (22.30, 23.20 and 23.35), Leeds (22.45) and Newcastle (23.55 and 01.00) would be getting ready for their departure times and close attention had to be paid to the progress of the empty stock which ran into Kings Cross from the various sidings around Wood Green behind the various types of Type 2 diesels we possessed.

It was at this time that any weakness in the supply of engines tended to show. From 16.00 onwards the balance of power was away from the division and until the up overnight trains started to arrive in the early hours there was only a small margin of flexibility in what could be used in the event of a failure.

Almost all the night trains were booked to be worked by Deltics. One exception was the 23.20 Edinburgh sleeper which although making only one intermediate call - Newcastle - in its 393 mile trip consisted of only seven or eight vehicles and was one of the few services still to be entrusted to a Class 40. If a train failed in the London area the usual practice was to get hold of the nearest Type 2 and haul

cies - would be sent up at full speed to rescue the stranded train and haul it north.

More often than not drivers of labouring engines, knowing that delivery lay in the hands of New England, tried to keep going and would give a prearranged whistle code on passing Huntingdon (or Essendine in the up direction) which allowed us to send a crew over to the pilot to get it up to the North station by the time the failure arrived.

The fact that a class 47 did nothing at Peterborough but wait for one of its kin to break down gives some indication of the faith that diesels had engendered for themselves during their first years of service, although to be fair, the practise had not been introduced with dieselisation but had existed in steam days when most of the major East Coast locations had maintained a main line engine - usually a V2 or A3 - for contingency purposes.

Speaking from memory I don't think I can recall a single shift when the services of the pilot was not used and as soon as it did disappear on an errand of mercy, it became a matter of priority to find another Class 47 which could fill the vacuum.

Different types had varying degrees of availability but the worst - by a long margin - in those days were the engines now known as the Class 47s. To say they were poor would be to understate matters and of the 50-odd that we had on our books, I cannot recall a time when more than 50% were at work. Indeed the doyenne of the class, D1500, as it then was, stayed in Crewe works for my entire eighteen month stay of tenure.

The English Electric main line engines were, to a marked degree, far more reliable that those of other manufacturers and although we had lost our original allocation of Class 40s to the Great Eastern, there were still a lot of them around from Gateshead, York and Haymarket sheds and they gave very little trouble. Indeed they were preferred for fast goods traffic since they seemed to get trains through the Arlesey, Sandy and Huntingdon bottlenecks far more smartly than the class 47s and when one of these trains was a minute or two short of a margin, if a class 40 was at the head the section controller would invariably instruct the signalman give it a run. (Such risks were not things to be taken lightly. The GN was pretty fastidious about time lost by express passenger services and to cause delay - even of a minute or two - was to invite trouble later on when the running sheets were inspected. The DCCs at Kings Cross were not normally given to covering up the sins of their staff and could be pretty caustic with any controllers who had either caused delay to a train or had failed to prevent someone doing likewise. Equally those who played safe through policies of caution were equally berated. Risks were encour-

MALLARD meets MASTER CUTLER in Parsifal's day on the GN. As the text relates, the new diesels were treated more or less as steam 'but different' and some working details (pilot provision for example) did not radically change for a long time. Take a minor thing like shed plates - they were affixed to diesels although they served no practical purpose because of the rigid diesel control system and it may be presumed that their eventual demise owed something to the attentions of collectors, who found their removal a simple matter to arrange. Photograph P.Ransome-Wallis.

the whole thing to Peterborough where the Class 47 pilot would take over. If, on the other hand, the failure occurred well north of Hitchin the pilot - a Clarence Yard 47 which stood spare at New England for such contingen-

TABLE 4.	WORKINGS OF D9003 'MELD'	
DATE	SERVICE	MILEAGE
30/3/66	11.00 EDINBURGH - KINGS CROSS	393
	20.20 KINGS CROSS - EDINBURGH	786
31/3/66	10.00 EDINBURGH - KINGS CROSS	1179
	20.20 KINGS CROSS - EDINBURGH	1572
1/4/66	08.00 EDINBURGH - KINGS CROSS	1965
	16.00 KINGS CROSS - EDINBURGH	2358
	23.55 EDINBURGH - KINGS CROSS	2751
2/4/66	12.00 KINGS CROSS - EDINBURGH	3144
	22.50 EDINBURGH - KINGS CROSS	3537
DAILY AVERAGE : 884 MILES		

Headboards, such as that ilustrated, died out with the arrival of diesels whose turn-rounds were often too brief to permit the fitting of such luxuries. Occasionally the locomotive of the Master Cutler Pullman would sport a headboard whilst the Flying Scotsman had a special 'thistle' design which appeared on the odd occasion its existence was remembered. The example shown in the photograph is of particular interest to the writer since it remains in his possession as a momento of his days at Kings cross. 3rd September 1957.

aged provided they were calculated and - above all - successful. At the end of the day the accounts of running were inspected - in detail - by Bill Stirling (sir) and he had no qualms about making his feelings known where poor working was concerned.

The Deltics, which of course were from the English Electric stud, were reliable by any standards which, since they hauled the majority of services from Kings Cross, was no bad thing. That however is not to say that they were completely trouble free as Table 1 indicates, in a sample week from 1966.

The mileages worked by the Deltics were quite astonishing in relation to what we were historically accustomed to. The Pacifics had done pretty well to exceed 400 miles a day - the single (summer only) non-stop to Edinburgh or a couple of round trips to Grantham - whilst the Deltics were more than doubling that figure. D9003, considered one of the poorer specimens, in the first four days of the week in question worked the following services until it failed on arrival, with some unrecorded defect, at Kings Cross on the Friday morning. Whatever the fault

A Brush type 4 receives a transplant at Clarence Yard during a visit in March 1965. One wonders what the fitter and his mate are doing thirty years on. One of the difficulties experienced by BR during the 1960s revolved around the excellent quality of apprenticeships provided and the fact that as soon as many qualified, they were snapped up - by dint of higher wages - by the motor industry.

The English Electric 2000hp type 4s (Class 40) were an attractive engine, visually and aurally, but lacked the power needed to time GN services and in 1966 an instruction was issued barring them from all the principal workings out of Kings Cross. In view of this restriction it seemed surprising that the GN's west coast rival used the same class for all its workings out of Euston, especially as something very much more powerful was needed to recover from the electrification slacks that the LNW suffered from during the first half of the 1960s. In this view the driver of D201 looks back along No.10 platform for the right away on 9 July 1958, not long after the introduction of the class to the Great Northern.

was it cannot have been of a major nature since the engine resumed work the following Sunday by taking out the 09.40 Harrogate Sunday Pullman to Leeds Central.

The fact that only half the class - eleven out of twenty two locomotives - completed the week without being stopped in some way, gives a rather distorted picture since only a few of

the failures resulted in engines being out of traffic for any length of time. D9009, for example, failed at York early on the Wednesday morning whilst working the 22.30 Kings Cross - Edinburgh yet was back in traffic a few hours later when it took over the 13.00 Kings Cross - Newcastle from the booked class 47, returning to London with the Up Flying Scotsman the following day. Only three Deltics, including D9009, actually failed in traffic (i.e. caused delay to a train) and these shortcomings involved D9014 which on the Saturday failed whilst working the 07.45 Kings Cross - Leeds Central 'flyer' and had to be assisted by D1540, and D9013 which had to be rescued by D5602 whilst running through the GN suburban area. Interestingly, each of these engines were representatives of each of the three depots to which the class was allocated - the other failures arose from defects discovered during examinations and caused no delay to services.

Many of the failures in traffic were due to the train heating boilers which were notoriously difficult to keep going unless the second man concerned had an especial devotion to duty. If a boiler failed at any time the driver was required to ask for a replacement engine and failures from this source tended to give an inaccurate assessment of the locomotive as a pulling unit.

The train heating saga was nonsensical in some respects since in the majority of cases - and especially when a train was made up of Mk 1 stock - it made little difference to the passenger whether or not the boiler was working. Those in the know soon discovered that the most effective way of keeping warm on the East Coast was to close the doors and windows of a compartment and to chain smoke furiously for the first couple of hours. This was usually more effective in raising the temperature than train heating boiler which few firemen ever succeeded in getting to work efficiently.

It was a pity that this aspect of operations was never seriously tackled. In the mid-sixties the East Coast operated trains that were amongst the fastest and most frequent in the world and probably the most punctual. For five hours or so one would be whisked at very high speeds up the main line, shivering all the way and anticipating an early arrival at Kings Cross where one could go in seek of warmth. At somewhere around Hitchin, however, the driver would decide that the train heating boiler was inactive and would stop for a replacement engine. A Class 31 or Baby Deltic - with an equally ineffective boiler - would be coupled on with absolutely no positive result beyond condemning the near-frozen passengers to thirty extra minutes.

Conversely the LNW main line, which at the time was a shambles because of the drawn-out electrification scheme, did succeed in warming its

Between the tunnels 1. A Clarence Yard Deltic heads for home with the 10.15 Newcastle - Kings Cross. Although the policy of the day was opposed to the naming of engines an exception was made in the case of the Deltics, the GN allocation continuing the tradition of receiving racehorse names.

Between the tunnels 2. A Gateshead 2000hp type 4 splutters the 10.20 Kings Cross - Leeds/Bradford express up the gradient towards Woolmer Green during May 1963, the last season in which these engines were booked to work this service; Deltics took over by the following year.

passengers where electric heating was in force and on several occasions I well remember being at Edinburgh Waverley waiting for an up overnight to Kings Cross and, remembering the cold of the previous journey, jumping into a Carstairs service and travelling to Euston because at least the train would be well heated between Crewe and Nuneaton.

Although the Deltics were given extraordinarily complex cyclic diagrams no attempt was made to keep to them - I cannot recall the workings ever being referred to - although it was regarded as de rigeur to book a Deltic to a Deltic-hauled service. Generally an engine would return on the next working of whatever it happened to come in to Kings Cross on, irrespective of whether it was a Gateshead engine on a (theoretical) Haymarket turn. On the occasions that the heathen North sent up a Type 4 on a Deltic service, great efforts would be made by two out of the three power controllers to see that a Deltic was allocated to the return service and it was unusual, although

not unknown, to see a Type 4 deputising for a Deltic. As in days of old, Stirlings' (the other one) dictum that a train with two engines was like a man with two wives held good and it was rare to see a passenger train with more than one engine. However on the Thursday before Good Friday for a number of years in the mid-1960s, a Deltic was required for some purpose at York and to get one there, an additional engine was diagrammed to double head 1A58, the 19.30 Aberdonian. On most occasions the working never materialised as it was found possible to make alternative arrangements but in one instance - I think it was 1966 - the train was double headed and the roar from the two engines - 6,600hp - as they climbed through Copenhagen and Gasworks was something that might have given Wagner food for thought.

Out of the 42 main line departures from Kings Cross, it was fortunate that only 15 were booked to Class 47 locomotives. Had it been more then we should have been in serious trouble

since the class seemed unable to stand up to sustained high speed running although when put on Deltic services they usually kept the point to point timings provided they were not called upon to recover delays.

One train that seemed prone to delay north of Grantham - probably at Doncaster where they appeared never to know the difference between a timetable and a calendar - was 1A23, the 08.00 Morning Talisman from Edinburgh. If it passed Stoke more than a few minutes behind time the section controller would ask what the engine was and told "a Deltic" then the main line would be cleared with more than the usual degree of efficiency to give it a run. To look over the section controllers shoulder, where the progress of the train was graphed in relation to its path, and to see the Deltic literally eat up the lost time, was something that put a capital M into Morale. If the train had a class 47 on then making an especial effort to keep the line clear was a waste of time since the best they could do was to maintain the running times.

In 1966 D9001 - which always seemed to be selected for such purposes - was tried for a week on a series of very high speed tests culminating in the Leeds flyer which left Kings Cross at 15.55 on a 162 minute schedule to Leeds Central, including a stop at Wakefield. This was about twenty minutes better than the previous Diesel best and a Deltic was considered essential from the moment the train started to run. In parenthesis, I recall riding on the footplate of D9000 with the service on the third day of operation, an experience which confirmed the generally held view that D9000 was a laggard. At no point could the speed be induced to rise above 102 m.p.h. and a late arrival, thanks to a prolonged signal stand at Doncaster - where else - was recorded at Leeds. Encouraging as this new timing was, it was nonetheless disturbing to learn that it was neither faster nor heavier than the West Riding streamliner which had been in operation thirty years earlier and could probably, given the professional resolution that existed at Kings Cross, have been handled by an A4 where they would have been better employed than footling about on the Caledonian where the survivors at that time had been put to pasture.

One afternoon a class 47 came up in the diagram and where his colleagues would have moved heaven and earth to find a Deltic replacement, the Hornsey Loafer, perhaps in a liverish frame of mine, declared that the thing could return 'as booked'. We, the assistants, in gleeful expectation of seeing the Loafer brought to justice in an uncomfortable interview on the subject of punctuality, could hardly wait for the train to get to Leeds so that we could find out how much time had been lost by the Type 4. I was appointed to ring Leeds Central and was

The Up Master Cutler, complete with headboard, prepares to leave Retford on a misty April day in 1959 behind 2000hp diesel-electric D209. Although powered by Clarence Yard locomotives, the train was worked by Darnall men who, under an agreement made to smooth the introduction of the working (which was seen as a threat to the security of the GC route), were not obliged to work through if the diesel failed and a steam engine was substituted.

rather chagrined to learn that the train had arrived on time.

The Loafer - knowing full well that we had desired nothing more than his exile to Siberia or (better still) Doncaster - smiled for the first time in our experience and remarked that since the 15.55 was only half a train (eight coaches) a J50 could have kept time with it.

I reflected afterwards that it was a fact that on many occasions I had recorded prestige services with a Deltic on the front, such as the 10.00 Scotsman and saw time kept without the speed ever rising above 90 m.p.h..

Most of our Class 47s spent more time in the works at Crewe than on East Coast metals and I am inclined to connect their poor availability with the amount of work the GN called upon them to do since other depots that had them in large numbers did not appear to suffer as we did. And I am bound to say that when I transferred to the Great Eastern after eighteen months at Kings Cross, none of the 47s which were shared between Stratford and Norwich gave anything like the difficulties ex-

At the time of this photograph, 28 November 1960, main line diesels were still something of a curiosity at Kings Cross although extensive preparations for the invasion were under way as can be deduced from the half-completed examination shed being constructed in the passenger loco. Prior to dieselisation the loco yard was used for preparing turn-round engines for the return leg of their workings whilst, afterwards, it was used by almost all main line engines arriving at Kings Cross.

By the banks of the Ouse. An English Electric type 4 slows for the 70 mph speed restriction through Offord & Buckden; a short respite from the fast running down the bank from Stevenage and the stiff climb between Peterborough and Abbots Ripton. The train concerned is the 13.00 Kings Cross - Edinburgh 'Heart of Midlothian' and the date is 1 August 1958.

perienced at Kings Cross. This is probably because the work they performed on the Great Eastern was far less intensive than that of the GN.

To demonstrate the work that the Clarence Yard Class 47s were expected to fulfill, Table 2 gives a week's cycle of workings which, it will be seen, kept

the engine continuously occupied in a wide variety of duties. After completing the eight day working shown - which excludes any reference to the Sunday which would have intervened at some point - the engine then spent a number of days working 75-wagon coal trains between New England and Ferme Park.

Amongst other things the workings show how very insular the railways still were at that time; the class 47 hardly strayed away from GN metals, the exception being Leeds Central which, although historically a Great Northern location, had been ceded to the North Eastern Region shortly after nationalisation. The workings also indicate how much traffic there then was between Doncaster and Kings Cross and it is likely that, thirty years on, diagrammers today would be hard pressed to keep an engine fully occupied within the boundaries of the former GN.

Perhaps the most curious working was that of the second day when the engine worked the 02.00 to Grantham - one of a series of services, some of which ran only to Peterborough, known as 'parlies': an abbreviation for parliamentary - long distance stopping train. On reaching Grantham the train waited for the 20.20 Edinburgh to Kings Cross to arrive which brought up the dining car (and staff) that had worked as far as York in the 19.30 Aberdonian from Kings Cross the previous evening. This was coupled to the

D5303 in its early days, 1959, runs onto the passenger loco at Kings Cross between duties. Although not as unsuccessful as the North British and Baby Deltics, the BRCW 1160hp type 2s were ill-suited to the rigours of the GN suburban services and were eventually transferred to the Scottish region, D5303 going to Haymarket. The BRCW Type 2s survived in the north for many years on work of a less arduous nature. *Photograph Alec Swain.*

'parly' and taken to Lincoln where it formed the only through train of the day to Kings Cross.

Two days later the engine worked the XP64 stock - forerunner of the BR mark 11 vehicles - between Leeds and London, a working that called at all the major intermediate points in order to give as wide a variety of passengers as possible the opportunity to comment upon the experimental coaches. (After a few months on the Leeds run the coaches were transferred to the 08.00 Kings Cross - Edinburgh and 16.00 return, after which they were sent over to the Great Western, where they seemed to disappear from sight).

Other classes of Type 4 diesels were frequent visitors to Kings Cross although only one - apart from the first batch of class 40s - was ever allocated to the region; this was D168 which spent some time at New England ostensibly for crew training but in practice covering up for defective class 47s. The Class 40s worked many of the night goods services and appeared from time to time on passenger trains although only the 14.20 semi-fast to York and the 23.20 Edinburgh were actually diagrammed to them. (We did,

in fact, have an instruction that class 40 engines were not to be used on East Coast services if anything else could be found. The weight of trains - 11 to 14 coaches on most services - was beyond their time keeping capabilities).

By way of an aside, it always struck me as curious that our great rival, The LNW, had, until 1966, nothing better than the class 40, which could be seen on almost every express that left Euston for the north whilst the Midland - always the Cinderella of the LM - had an altogether more powerful class as the standard express type.

Class 46 engines (Cromptons) were regular visitors to the GN and seemed to work efficiently enough though they were too infrequently seen to form an accurate judgement. I do, however, remember an interesting night with D172 which got itself into the national press by failing at Biggleswade whilst working - in lieu of a Deltic - the 20.20 Edinburgh - Kings Cross. Baby Deltic D5906 was sent from Hitchin to assist and it was decided first of all to remove D172 from the train and park it in an adjacent siding. No sooner had D5906 started to haul the Type 4 off its train when the latter burst into flames caus-

ing all four roads to be blocked for about two hours. (It was a notable night, moreover, because the minute D172 started its immolation, D5623, class 31, working an up parcels train, became derailed on the main line at Grantham. Happy days). The earlier series of the Sulzer type 4s - later the class 45 - were 'Midland' and were regarded as a different engine from those of the later batch (Class 46) allocated to York and Gateshead and I can only recall one instance of a 'Midland' engine appearing in Kings Cross when the Leeds Division, for reasons unknown, gave a Holbeck driver a class 45 for a GN working. Upon arrival - the driver was not booked to return with his engine - it became stranded, for there were no Kings Cross drivers with the requisite traction knowledge and I believe that in the end arrangements had to be made for a Kentish Town man to drive the thing back to Leeds with a GN driver acting as his conductor.

Returning to the topic of high speed running, one particular sprint by a class 47 sticks in my mind following the discovery - and I cannot recall why or how - that the Leicester guard for

A particular feature of the east coast route which disappeared with steam. A4 Pacific 60032 GANNET of Kings Cross sets off with the 09.30 'Elizabethan' - known locally as the 'non-stop' - for Edinburgh; the longest through engine working in the country. Although the London and Edinburgh crews who worked the service took a considerable pride in the working, they could not be induced to continue the tradition with diesels and thus the service ceased in 1962.

Perhaps in anticipation of an easy days work, the fireman - sporting a white collar and buttonhole - of D206 enjoys a joke with an inspector at Kings Cross before setting off with an additional train on 24 October 1959. The driver, checking the coupling operation at the rear of the engine, has turned up in more orthodox clothing.

the 00.05 St Pancras - Leeds happened to find himself at Peterborough North about an hour and a half before he was due to leave with his train from London. The DCC asked me if anything could be done and, believing in living dangerously, I utilised the passenger pilot to run the guard up to Kings Cross. The engine left Peterborough at 23.00 and every effort was made to give it a clear run. I cannot recall the time it reached London but St Pancras later reported that the 00.05 had left to time. (St Pancras, although only feet away from the Cross, represented a different nation. One of their people once wandered into the control who have a look around and we stared at him as though he had come from China).

One type 4 diesel that had happier associations with the GN was the solitary DP2 which, after starting its career on the LNW came across to Clarence Yard, initially to work the Sheffield Pullman service and latterly the 12.00 Kings Cross - Edinburgh, returning with one of the up sleepers. I cannot recall that this engine - which admittedly had the support of a full time fitter - gave us many problems apart from one instance when it gave up the ghost whilst hauling the 12.00 Glasgow over the Stilton Fen bottleneck and caused quite severe delays. A few years later the engine was involved - whilst working the same service - in the Thirsk mishap where it received such serious damage that it was withdrawn from traffic. It is curious to think that the class 50s - which I believe gave some severe mechanical headaches - were bred from DP2.

Very early days apart, the smaller

diesels did not give much trouble and the Class 31s in particular did everything required of them although when diesels first appeared on the local services it was a very different story and neither the North British D6100 class

or the Baby Deltics did what was intended of them.

At one time all peak services, except one, from Hertford North were booked to be worked by the North British engines. Chaos broke out every morning - until things changed - because the passengers ignored the diesel services which were not only uncertain but unheated - and attempted to board the exception, a Gresley quin hauled by an LMS 2-6-0. The resulting overcrowding had to be seen to be believed.

One verdict on the new Type 2s - as succinct as any - came from one of the loco controllers who suggested that they would only be of use if the tops were removed and the insides filled with coal so that they could be worked from New England to Ferme Park (by an Austerity, naturally) as high capacity coal wagons. (A few years later this transformation was being advocated for all diesels).

The Baby Deltics were at first no better and had to be withdrawn from traffic for a protracted period, returning in 1964 to lead a trouble-free and useful existence, working most of the diagrams based upon Hitchin. The chief problem with the rebuilds was that 1100hp was insufficient for most demands and when they worked the Cambridge Buffets - one was diagrammed for a time to the 15.35 Kings Cross to Cambridge - punctuality was touch and go since the slightest signal check was beyond their powers of recovery. They were however very use-

A quiet moment at the Cross. Standing in platform 10 with 55 minutes to prepare for departure is the 12.05 Queen of Scots Pullman for Glasgow (Queen Street) via Leeds and Harrogate whilst B1 4-6-0 61334 kills time in platform 5 after arriving with the 09.18 buffet express from Cambridge. The train of stock due next in platform 7 was a useful working for Tynesiders with a sense of speed and economy since it left London five minutes after the Pullman yet reached Newcastle eleven minutes earlier - without any supplementary fare.

Final triumph. Diesels at Finsbury Park early in 1965.

ful on the inner suburban services and it often amused me to stand at the south end of Wood Green to watch one of these engines rush down from Harringay, flat out to get a run up Potters Bar tunnel, looking spanking new at the head of ten pretty disreputable Gresley articulated non-corridor vehicles. The class 20s which were, in effect, allocated to Hatfield, were reserved for local goods workings and, because they lacked train heating apparatus, were not diagrammed for any passenger work. We did, however, when weather conditions permitted and shortage of power dictated, use them occasionally on inner suburban duties and I recall on at least one occasion riding up to town behind one during the morning peak.

One type of engine that gave very little cause for concern were the 350hp pilots (Class 08) of which more than thirty were scattered around the Kings Cross and Peterborough areas. Each morning - if they remembered - the running foremen at Hornsey and New England would rattle off the numbers of engines in each working and that would be all one heard of them for twenty-four hours. I cannot recall any difficulties arising from these engines and the same has to be said for the curious 204hp pilots that could be found at Hitchin.

Looking back after the passage of nearly three decades it was both an interesting and depressing period in history. It was interesting in the sense that a novel form of motive power with a high theoretical availability and capability was being pitted against the traction we were far more familiar with, whilst it was depressing to see trains being continually disrupted because of the difficulty the newcomers had in completing a days work.

How we got through those early years was probably due to the generous spare capacity that had been provided in the allocation of engines; something based partly on LNER tradition and partly on lack of experience.

Given the requirement of, say, 15 daily diagrams to cover, the optimum number of engines to provide is a question, eventually, of experience. If the engines can be relied upon then perhaps 17 or 18 will suffice to cover for examinations and the occasional contingency. Thirty years ago however there was no background of experience from which to draw and it was our good fortune that someone had ordered more diesels than we should ever have been able to use. (Had the 47s worked as intended, it is probable that half the sidings on the GN would have been cluttered up with unemployed locomotives waiting for the chance to get on the front of a train).

One aspect in which history did play a positive, if somewhat wasteful, role was the steam practice of maintaining spare engines all over the place; a habit that was perpetuated well into the 1960s. New England, for example, was host to Clarence Yard diagram 27 which required a class 47 to stand idle in case it was needed to replace a main line failure. The LNER had been a believer in expensive contingencies and it was a tradition for which we were grateful. Indeed, given the number of times a day the pilot (as it was known) was called upon to go to the rescue, it is difficult to know how we should have been placed without it. Even so, despite the existence of the pilots, we still had to cancel a lot of mineral services in order to keep passenger trains running. I never kept a record of failures - something I regret - but I do owe my keyboard skills to the fact that one of

my duties on the night shift was to type the return of main line locomotive failures. It was generally a good hour's work.

Eventually the gravity of the situation became apparent to someone in the high command who - belatedly it seemed to us - put some thought into producing a formula that would keep the worst of the engines, the class 47s, at work and towards the end of the 1960s attention began to focus on shortfalls in maintenance.

An analysis revealed that relatively few engines were being presented for a daily inspection because the system of weekly examinations required a depot to look at an engine that was in a particular working rather than to seek out individual locomotives. This meant - because engines were failing to keep to their diagrams - that some engines were examined several times a week whilst others went unnoticed.

A scheme was therefore introduced in 1968 which required the engine controllers in each division to introduce a ticket system for each locomotive, each engine ticket being endorsed with the day and time the engine was due for a weekly examination. (F4, for example, meant that the engine had to be sent to a depot for a weekly examination by 14.00 on Friday). The system also included daily examinations and ensured that engines were seen systematically and not, as had been the case, haphazardly.

Engine failures on the East coast were not eradicated by any means but the scheme did bring about a noticeable improvement and it was probably the greatest single advance made by the Eastern Region in regard to diesel locomotive availability since their inception. Had it been introduced with the engines a decade earlier not only would life have been a good deal easier in general but it is possible that some of the classes, condemned as unsatisfactory, might have performed as the makers had intended.

It was not only the motive power that started to change all those years ago. I remember quite vividly the people I worked with and the way they worked. By any standards they were single minded and their subject was their railway - always referred to by its pre-1923 title. I never once heard reference made to the LNER or LMS. This was generally the case, I believe, with most railwaymen up to that time but it was especially true of Kings Cross. Almost all those in the control system had come up through the grades - firemen, signalmen, yard and station inspectors, etc - with the result that the control organisation had an uncanny feel for what was going on outside. And because of that experience the confidence to give instructions was inherent and kept the railway on its toes, in marked contrast with today, in which decision making and self confidence have wilted in Governmental grip.

ORANGE WALKS SPECIALS

by
PAUL ANDERSON
&
W.A.C.SMITH

Little known outside Central Scotland even in their heyday, the specials provided for the annual Orange processions were big business for British Railways throughout the 1950s and early 1960s. The venue varied from year to year and freight only lines together with closed passenger stations were sometimes used. 'Orange Walks' have always been lively affairs and the train journeys were an integral part of the proceedings.

The Orange Society was formed as a secret Protestant order in Ireland during 1795 and was named after William, Prince of Orange who, as King William III, had defeated the Catholic King James II at the Battle of the Boyne in 1690. Orange lodges - local groupings of the society - spread throughout Ireland and eventually into Great Britain and many parts of the British empire. Annual processions have been held on or around July 12th to commemorate the Battle of the Boyne ever since, despite official attempts to discourage them. Religious and political

The 4.55pm return Orange special from Greenock Princes Pier to Bellgrove on 9th July 1955 was hauled by Parkhead V1 2-6-2T No.67661. This was a heavy nine coach train and Standard 2-6-4T No.80023 was attached as pilot for the punishing climb through tunnels beneath Greenock and along the hillside to Upper Port Glasgow. After the descent from Devol Moor and easier gradients beyond Kilmacolm, the pilot was removed at Bridge of Weir. On seeing the double-header, an elderly Corkerhill driver was heard to make disparaging remarks about 'North British' engines and men! However, in an attempt to improve timekeeping of the morning business trains out of Princes Pier, the operating authorities had to resort to pairs of ex-Caledonian 4-4-0s during the early 1950s. In this view of the south end of Princes Pier station, the closed stairways from Greenock's main street can be seen through the smoke haze.

Junior Orange Walks are held about a month before the main procession and on 16th June 1956 eight specials were provided from various Glasgow stations for a gathering at East Kilbride. All were worked by Class 5 tender locos to obviate watering difficulties, and class 3MT Mogul No.77008 acted as a standby at Busby in case of unforeseen problems. Standard 4-6-0 No.73056 of 66A Polmadie shed made an all out effort as it took the single line at Busby with special No.6 before tackling the curving 1 in 57 gradient ahead.

considerations apart, the parades are colourful occasions and popular spectator events. As many as 50 lodges take part in a single march and are identified by their huge banners measuring up to twenty feet square. They are led by the mace bearer who tosses his staff high in the air, retrieving it in moves worthy of an accomplished gymnast. Flutes, pipes, snare drums and kettledrums provide the accompaniment, but the noisiest instruments are undoubtedly the huge lambeg drums which are beaten incessantly. Orange Walks are held in the West of Scotland, Ayrshire, Fife and the Lothians on the Saturday before July 12th, and lodges gather at a predetermined venue, usually a public park or other open space. When rail was the main means of transport, a march to and from the local station was an important part of the ritual. Lodges departed from one station and often returned to another, followed by a parade through tenement lined streets to the original joining point. Partick and Maryhill stations in Glasgow were used in this way for example. At the gathering itself, participants relaxed and took refreshments as they listened to speeches.

The sheer scale of railway operations can be judged by events on 8th July 1950. For a massive demonstration at Darnley Park no less than 22 special trains converged on Kennishead station between Glasgow and Barrhead and nearby

Thornliebank on the East Kilbride branch. On the same day eight specials from Fife, the Lothians and Lanarkshire arrived at Bannockburn just south of Stirling for a rally at the famous battlefield site. The station had closed seven months previously on 2nd January, but was still in a fit state to be used. In 1951 fifteen specials came into Edinburgh Princes Street and a further five were received at Haymarket for a march to King's Park

On 6th July 1957 the Orange Walk at Broxburn in West Lothian generated four specials to Uphall station east of Bathgate, which had closed on 9th January 1956. They originated at Airdrie and Coatbridge, and each consisted of nine non-corridor coaches. Motive power was surprisingly varied, comprising B1 4-6-0 No.61396, Black 5 No.44702, Ivatt Mogul No.43135 and J37 0-6-0 No.64618. The last return working, due away from Uphall at 5.50pm and destined for Coatbridge Sunnyside, is seen passing Bathgate Upper some 25 minutes late behind No.64618. On the right, Class J36 0-6-0 No.65344 waited to bank a freight up to Armadale, two and a half miles to the west. Bathgate Upper station also closed in 1956. Veering away in the foreground is the line through Bathgate Lower to Slamannan and Airdrie North. Most of this was part of the old Slamannan Railway which dated from the early 1840s and lost its meagre passenger service on 1st May 1930.

| \multicolumn{7}{c}{DEPARTURES PRINCES PIER (17.12 to 19.23)} | | | | | | |
Train No.	Loco	Shed	Depart (Booked)	Depart (Actual)	Remarks	
192	67661	65C (Parkhead)	16.55	17.12	9 coaches.	
	80023	66A (Polmadie)			Pilot to 67661. Worked to Bridge of Weir and returned light engine for 18.15 departure.	
127	80000	67A (Corkerhill)	17.05	17.26	8 coaches	
128	42123	67A (Corkerhill)	17.13	17.32	8 coaches	
130	42245	66A (Polmadie)	17.22	17.49	8 coaches	
-	42238	66D (Greenock P.Pier)	17.27	17.43	Service train	
133	80026	66A (Polmadie)	17.40	18.02	8 coaches	
134	42190	67A (Corkerhill)	17.49	18.12	8 coaches	
137	80008	67A (Corkerhill)	17.58	18.38	9 coaches. Delay caused by station pilot requiring assistance with empty stock	
138	77009	66A (Polmadie)	18.07	18.50	8 coaches	
-	80023	66A (Polmadie)	18.15	18.30	Service train	
139	42206	65B (St Rollox)	18.20	19.00	7 coaches	
140	80054	66A (Polmadie)	18.35	19.07	7 coaches	
141	42247	66A (Polmadie)	18.43	19.16	8 coaches	
142	42275	66A (Polmadie)	18.52	19.23	6 coaches	

tually the end however, and passengers bound for Orange Walks today are easily absorbed by Strathclyde's frequent electric services.

Back in the bounteous days, BR's contribution to the celebrations of 9th July 1955 are worth examining in some detail as an insight into the achievements and difficulties of an Orange day operation. It was a glorious summer of unbroken sunshine and the march took place at Greenock, the first to be held there since 1938. Seventeen specials headed for the Clyde Coast, twelve of them arriving at Lynedoch station in the upper part of the town, the rest terminating at Greenock Central. The Lynedoch trains returned from grandiose Greenock Princes Pier station, but none of

In pouring rain on 11th July 1959, Edinburgh St. Margarets J39 0-6-0 No.64795, which was fresh out of Cowlairs Works, stormed away from Balloch Central with the last of nine Orange Walk Specials returning from the Bonnie Banks of Loch Lomond. Other motive power that afternoon included Class 5 4-6-0s Nos.44973 and 45458 from Fort William and Perth South sheds respectively, Moguls 76004 and 76100, Standard tanks 80054 and 80056, Stanier 2-6-2T No.40152 and V1 2-6-2T No.67671. The train is passing Forth & Clyde Junction signal box where the straggling rural line from Stirling, Buchlyvie and Drymen came in. It closed to passengers on 1st October 1934.

on 7th July. This particular assembly was attended by a thousand Orangemen from Belfast; they had crossed from Larne to Stranraer on M.V. PRINCESS VICTORIA and were taken forward to Glasgow by three special trains. The ill-fated vessel was to sink off Belfast Lough with heavy loss of life on 31st January 1953. Larkhall, south of Hamilton, was the venue in 1952 and Irvine in Ayrshire was chosen for the 1953 march. In 1954 twenty one trains were provided between Buchanan Street and Maryhill Central for a meet in Glasgow. Over the next

decade specials ran to Greenock (1955), East Kilbride (1956), Hamilton (1957), Stevenston near Ardrossan (1958), Balloch on Loch Lomond (1959), Larkhall again (1960), Paisley (1961), Motherwell (1962), Greenock again (1963), Ardrossan (1964) and Shotts (1965). The Glasgow & South Western Division Commercial Report of 1963 noted that the Orange specials to Greenock yielded a profit of just £130 and it is therefore somewhat surprising that nine trains were run to Ardrossan the following year and six went to Shotts in 1965. This was vir-

them left on time. In the case of Special 137, the problem was caused by station pilot No.54492 being unable to lift the empty stock out of Albert Harbour goods sidings until assisted by No.80008. The gradient out of the depot, which stood adjacent to Princes Pier passenger station, was 1 in 50 - hence the ex-Caledonian 4-4-0's difficulties with nine (albeit empty) coaches from a standing start. However, the passengers themselves were mainly responsible for delays. Most of them had indulged in copious liquid refreshment

(cont. page 51)

Saturday 9th July 1960 was a marvellous day for Orange Walk trains and fine sunny weather with a touch of cloud scudding in on a westerly breeze helped enliven the scene. Under the watchful eyes of permanent way men who had clamped the points, Standard Class 4MT 2-6-0 No.76002 made a robust start from Ross Yard with the 9.56am special from Motherwell to Larkhall East. Passengers and crew alike were clearly relishing the occasion and there was a certain amount of banter with their companions on the 9.36am special from Glasgow Central to Larkhall Central, headed by Standard 2-6-4T No.80057 waiting for the road south. The complex track layout is illustrated by this view. Mogul No.76002 had come in from the right distance over the Lesmahagow Railway which opened from Motherwell to Lesmahagow (later renamed Brocketsbrae) for mineral traffic on 1st December 1856, providing passenger services from 1st January 1868. On the other hand No.80057 had approached from the left distance over the line from Hamilton and Haughhead Junction; this had opened on 18th September and 2nd October 1876 for goods and passengers respectively and burrowed under the Lesmahagow Railway. Behind the camera at Ferniegair Junction, their paths crossed again, the Mogul continuing on the original Lesmahagow line and the tank taking the later Mid-Lanark route to the west.

B1 4-6-0 No.61117 dipped under the Hamilton-Lanark road about one and a quarter miles south of Ross Yard with the 10.35am Orange special from Bellgrove to Larkhall Central on 9th July 1960. For over 40 years this was the site of Merryton Junction, where the Mid-Lanark line to Stonehouse, Strathaven, Blackwood and Alton Heights (on the left) parted company with the original Lesmahagow Railway (on the right). The former opened on 1st June 1905. In 1949 Merryton Junction was abolished and the point of divergence moved north to Ferniegair Junction. Passenger services over the Lesmahagow Railway ceased on 10th September 1951 and those using the Mid-Lanark lines finished on 4th October 1965.

This panoramic view from an abandoned colliery bing west of Highlees on 9th July 1960 shows Standard 2-6-4T No.80027 toiling up the grass-grown Lesmahagow Railway, by then partly abandoned and singled, with the 10.22am special from Port Glasgow to Larkhall East. Old spoil heaps and derelict land marking the site of sidings and former mine property are all around. Merryton Junction was in the middle distance near the clump of trees, a large plantation near Riccarton forms the skyline on the left and ground slopes down to Clydesdale on the right.

On 6th July 1963 the Orange Walk was held at Greenock's Battery Park. Five specials from Glasgow St. Enoch and one from Bellgrove ran to Lynedoch station which had closed on 2nd February 1959, with the return journeys commencing at Greenock Princes Pier. Others originating at Bridgeton Cross, Parkhead Stadium, Cambuslang, Motherwewll and Kennishead came into Greenock Central and left from Fort Matilda. One of the Lynedoch trains, the ten coach 10.10am from Glasgow St. Enoch, is seen climbing away from Kilmacolm with Standard Mogul No.76091 and Standard 2-6-4T No.80030 in charge. Other pairings were 76092 with 80048; 80021 with 76095; 80052 with 73122 and 80053 with 76094. The Bellgrove train had English Electric Type I diesel No.D8099 on a reduced load of seven coaches. Return workings were delayed when a train was stoned near Cartsburn tunnel shortly after leaving Princes Pier.

It was still bright and sunny at the end of the day's proceedings on 9th July 1960 as Fairburn 2-6-4T No.42055 left Larkhall East with the 5.10pm return special to Motherwell. The station was somewhat remotely situated on the north east side of the town, although this area was once a hive of industrial activity - as indicated by the old mine workings to the right. At this time, the simple main building - identified by its steeply pitched roof - still overlooked the abandoned up platform. Until 1951 passenger trains continued along the west side of Clydesdale through Dalserf, Netherburn, Tillietudlem and Auchenheath to Bocketsbrae. On the far side of the valley, the Caledonian main line headed south towards Carstairs.

49

The last walk when steam traction predominated on specials was at Ardrossan on 11th July 1964. Six trains from Glasgow St. Enoch and one from Bellgrove ran to Ardrossan Town station whilst another two from Parkhead Stadium and Flemington near Motherwell arrived at Ardrossan Montgomerie Pier on the former Lanarkshire & Ayrshire system. Each train consisted of nine vehicles, mainly non-corridor, and most of the stock was stabled in the harbour sidings where Class 2 Mogul No.46413 was provided for pilot duties. Standard 2-6-4Ts worked six of the specials, with English Electric Type 1 D8100 on the Bellgrove train and Class 5 4-6-0 No.73120 and Mogul No.76114 on the St. Enoch services. 2-6-4T No.80005 is seen passing Castlehill Junction in brilliant sunshine with the 4.42pm return special from Ardrossan Town to Glasgow St. Enoch. The prominent knoll giving the junction its name rears above the railway to the right.

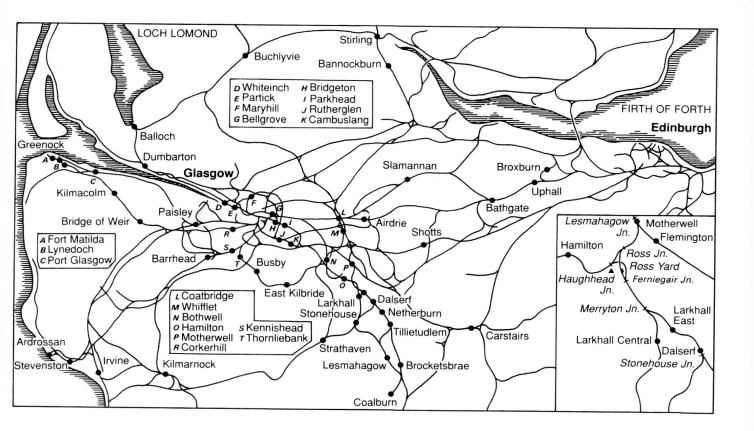

during the hot afternoon and boarding the train on time was a minor consideration! Nevertheless it was a happy occasion and railway staff responded flexibly.

Occasionally the Orange Walk specials used lines and stations closed to ordinary passenger traffic. On 6th July 1957 for example there was a walk at Broxburn in the grim oil shale mining area twelve miles to the west of Edinburgh. Four trains worked into Uphall station on the Bathgate line which had closed to passengers with the end of Edinburgh Waverley - Airdrie - Glasgow Queen Street Low Level services in 1956. Two specials came from Airdrie and the other pair originated at Coatbridge Sunnyside. However, the most interesting Orange day in post war years, from the railway point of view, was 9th July 1960. March organisers had chosen Larkhall in the hills above Clydesdale, four miles south of Hamilton, and fifteen specials used the town's two stations. Nine arrived at Larkhall Central, which remained open for local trains from Glasgow Central to Strathaven and Coalburn, but six terminated at Larkhall East, closed in 1951 with the end of Hamilton - Brocketsbrae services. Despite having been abandoned for nearly nine years, the former down platform was still in a fit state to receive passengers. There were six trains from Glasgow Central, two from Motherwell and others from Rutherglen, Bridgeton Cross, Parkhead Stadium, Partick West, Port Glasgow, Bellgrove and Greenock Princes Pier, the last of these returning to Cartsdyke to allow a final march through the town. Specials from Motherwell, Parkhead and

Bellgrove were routed via Ross Junction and Ferniegair Junction over the original 1856 Lesmahagow Railway route from Motherwell, which was eclipsed by the 1876 spur from Hamilton and Haughhead Junction as far as passenger services were concerned (see map for layout). The Bellgrove train also used a freight only connection between former North British and Caledonian metals at Whifflet. 'One engine in steam' working was suspended on the Larkhall East line and it was operated as a siding. Empty stock ran off to Dalserf and Netherburn further down the old Brocketsbrae line and locos took water at the former, where ex-Caledonian 0-6-0 No.57335 performed shunting duties from 9.30am. During the afternoon the Jumbo went to Larkhall Central where five trains were stabled, another being at Stonehouse with the remaining three venturing down to Strathaven. Engines from the trains stabled at Larkhall Central went back to the goods yard at Ross Junction for water. Return workings commenced with the 4.20pm from Larkhall East and finished with the 6.37pm from Larkhall Central.

Orange Walks Specials certainly took place in pre-war years but information is difficult to come by. However, on 8th July 1933 Bothwell on the LNER branch from Shettleston to Hamilton had trains from Parkhead, Bellgrove, Whiteinch Victoria Park (returning to Maryhill) and Dumbarton. There were also five from Glasgow Queen Street Low Level and one from Airdrie South which reversed at Sunnyside Junction to travel thence via Coatbridge Central and Bellshill. It was estimated that a total of 7,300 adults and 890 juve-

niles would be carried. No doubt there were specials into Bothwell LMS station as well, this being a terminus at the end of a short branch from Fallside on the main line between Newton and Motherwell. Bothwell LMS and LNER stations closed in 1950 and 1955 respectively. The town does not seem to have been considered as a post-war Orange Walk venue, perhaps because it was becoming a somewhat up-market housing area in the 1950s.

As a postscript, it is worth noting that despite making it easy for Orangemen to reach their destination, the specials sometimes helped to create chaos for ordinary travellers. The Walk at Stevenston near Ardrossan on 5th July 1958 generated eight specials to Saltcoats Central and a further nine to Stevenston Moor Park (closed to regular passenger services on 4th July 1932) on the nearby Lanarkshire & Ayrshire line to Montgomerie Pier. A large Irish contingent arrived by sea at Ardrossan harbour. There were no less than 80,000 participants, and the march was routed over the level crossing at Stevenston station on the Largs line to reach the shore. Considerable delay to services resulted with trains held on either side of the crossing until they could be hand signalled across together. Such was the congestion that evening that trains from the coast were running up to three hours late - the last did not reach Glasgow St. Enoch until after 1.0am, and buses and taxis had to be hired to get passengers home.

All photographs taken by W.A.C. Smith.

Good Morning ....
.......Campers !

Notes by
Andrew McRae

The LNER pioneered the use of camping coaches on Britain's railways when, in July 1933, it introduced ten newly converted ex-Great Northern Railway six wheelers for use at various locations in the north of England. Such was the haste of the refurbishment process, the vehicles at first appeared for use as camping coaches still bearing their service running numbers and the numerals identifying their previous employment as third class passenger accommodation. Conversion involved stripping out three of the original five compartment to create a kitchen and 'day compartment' whilst the remaining two compartments were left in situ to serve as bedrooms for the six campers. Coach No.42345, which in later seasons was identified as CC10, was initially used at Pateley Bridge.

Camping Coach memories, Brightlingsea, 1936.

The footboard and spring identify the vehicle in the background as one of the former Manchester, Sheffield and Lincolnshire six wheelers which comprised the bulk of the 1934 conversions. The letter A indicates that the coach lacks an inside corridor, in the fashion of all the first thirty five conversions. From 1935 onwards, new conversions allowed internal access, whilst those coaches already in use were suitably altered in due course to ensure that campers no longer had to climb along the footboard to move between compartments. A very comprehensive range of equipment was provided in the coaches, including more than one hundred and thirty items of cutlery, crockery and kitchen utensils. The campers pictured appear to be making a point of demonstrating the fact that, for some unknown reason, the extensive inventory did not feature a fish-slice! Someone in authority obviously noticed, for the following year this omission was duly rectified.

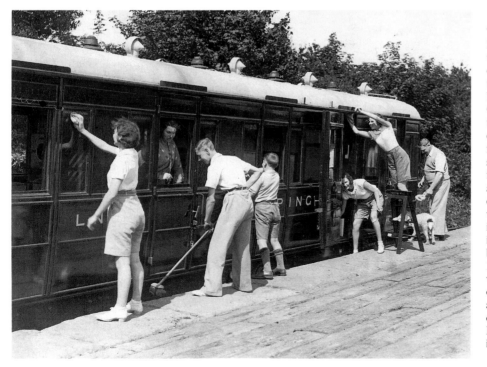

This busy party of campers, pictured at Forge Valley, appear to be taking to the extreme the request to return the coach to a clean and tidy condition for the benefit of the next group of holidaymakers! Coach No.CC17, formerly No.42492, is another ex-Great Northern Railway six wheeler built to Diagram No.245. The majority of the second batch of camping coaches were, in fact, former Manchester, Sheffield and Lincolnshire Railway six wheelers, but the twenty five new conversions sanctioned on 4th January 1934 did include a further six vehicles of Great Northern Railway origin. The coach was outshopped on 10th March 1934 displaying the revised livery; the previous teak finish remained but it now featured the bodyside legend 'LNER - Camping'. From 1935 onwards, all LNER camping coaches were repainted in the familiar green and cream tourist stock livery. This was similarly applied to all post-nationalisation camping coaches on the Eastern and North Eastern Regions and also, at a later stage, to those in use on the London Midland.

Fashion, glamour, and LNER Camping Coach No.13, converted from an ex-MS&LR third, at Hopton, 1934. The ethereal effect surrounding the coach and one of the campers is due to an amateur attempt to mask out the background.

Another early photograph depicts Coach No.42082, later to become CC5, at Cloughton. In both 1933 and 1934 when a further twenty five conversions were brought into use, it was possible to have a camping coach moved between different locations on particular branch lines during the course of a holiday. The 1934 LNER Camping Holidays Booklet identified eighty three locations on twenty eight different branches. In addition to Cloughton, both Staintondale and Robin Hood's Bay were featured locations on the Whitby to Scarborough section. The facility of moving between stations was not available from 1935 onwards, although a special seven berth 'Touring Camping Coach' with a fixed week-long itinerary, was introduced at this time. Coach No.42082 reveals that the inner of the two sleeping compartments housed four campers; the upper berths are visible through the windows whilst the end compartment served for a further two people.

The name of THE CORNISHMAN had its origins in late broad gauge days. At that time and until the advent of the as-then un-named THE CORNISH RIVIERA LIMITED in 1904, it ran between Paddington and Penzance. The name was revived in 1952 for a wholly different service between Wolverhampton and Penzance via Cheltenham and Stratford upon Avon. The up service is depicted here in charge of No.1010 COUNTY OF CAERNARVON heading a rake of new BR Mark I coaches in chocolate and cream livery. It was leaving Plymouth North Road on 4th July 1957, with 2-6-2T No.5506 at right fulfilling the duty of station pilot.

Western Region Named Trains in the West Country

Notes and Photographs by R.C.Riley.

The oldest of GWR named trains and the best known was the CORNISH RIVIERA LIMITED, a service introduced in 1904 but only named two years later when the Westbury cut-off was opened. This reduced the Paddington - Plymouth route from 245.7 miles to 225.7 miles, which was run non-stop in a few minutes over four hours. In some years known as the CORNISH RIVIERA EXPRESS, it carried its original title on 19th July 1956 when No.6017 KING EDWARD IV was hauling the up train past an almost deserted sea wall at Teignmouth. The eleven coach train was formed of BR Mark I stock in chocolate and cream livery, with a GWR restaurant car in the formation.

The TORBAY EXPRESS started before World War I and for a few years included a portion for Ilfracombe, slipped at Taunton. Immediately before the war it was re-timed ten minutes later to leave Paddington at 12 noon, with no slip portion and running non-stop to Exeter and thence fast to Torquay. In later years it was occasionally worked by a King 4-6-0, bringing the unusual sight of such an engine on the single line between Goodrington and Kingswear. Castle No.7000 VISCOUNT PORTAL was recorded at Whiteball Siding signal box, 4th September 1954 with the earlier style of train nameboard.

THE DEVONIAN, introduced as a through train in 1927, ran between Bradford Forster Square and Paignton. In common with most named trains, other than the CORNISH RIVIERA, the service ceased during the war and was re-introduced in 1946. Its average speed was higher on LMS lines than on those of the GWR, a point emphasised in this photograph of No.7029 CLUN CASTLE leaving the station stop at Dawlish on the up service 5th July 1957. CLUN CASTLE survives, now in double chimney form, on the Great Central Railway at Loughborough. This engine also carried the earlier style headboard. From 1967 the northern extremity of the service was altered to Bradford Exchange with a reversal at Leeds and it continued for some years with "Peak" class diesel haulage.

In the years 1955/7 several named trains were introduced by the Western Region as an excuse to repaint set trains into former GWR chocolate and cream livery. One of these was THE MAYFLOWER, up from Plymouth in the morning and down in the evening, not recorded here. The other was THE ROYAL DUCHY, introduced in 1955 on the existing 1.30pm Paddington - Penzance and 10am up train. The latter is seen here passing Stoneycombe Quarry, 3rd July 1957, in charge of Castle No.5049 EARL OF DEVON. Again it consists of BR Mark I coaches with a GWR restaurant car.

By chance Castle No.5074 WELLING-TON (named after a World War Two bomber) was seen passing Wellington, Somerset, 6th July 1957, in charge of the up TORBAY EXPRESS from Kingswear to Paddington.

Granges and Halls provided the most common motive power on the Cornish main line, but here is No.5023 BRECON CASTLE passing Menheniot on 16th July 1956, on the down CORNISH RIVIERA LIMITED. Note that the early style of BR train nameboard simply reads CORNISH RIVIERA.

With a prodigious amount of steam escaping from the safety valves, Castle 4-6-0 No.5071 SPITFIRE heads the down CORNISHMAN past a deserted sea wall at Teignmouth, July 19th 1956.

Approaching Lipson Junction, Plymouth, near the end of its non-stop four hour run, 6019 KING HENRY V was hauling the down CORNISH RIVIERA on 4th July 1957. Note Laira roundhouse at right. The train carried its original name and consisted of BR Mark 1 coaches, apart from a GWR restaurant car, all in chocolate and cream livery.

Passing Laira Junction, Plymouth, No.6016 KING EDWARD V heads the up ROYAL DUCHY, the stock BR Mark 1 coaches with a GWR restaurant car. Laira shed in the distance while at this time, 15th July 1958, the Saltash service was still operated by railmotor trains. Some typical trailer cars can be seen in the siding at right. In the immediate foreground there is a glimpse of the Lee Moor Tramway crossing, horse operated. Used less than ten times in 1956/7 and in 1959/60, it was used 14 times in 1958 - to maintain English China Clays' right of way. Presumably this was to aid negotiations with BR for compensation in the event of closure. Last used on 26th August 1960, it was very soon afterwards re-moved.

The Euston we remember.....solid, dignified, majestic and not a little mysterious. A station which personified the Victorian desire for grandeur and which, up to the time of its rebuilding on the 1960s, was an impressive starting or finishing point for a long distance journey.

It did not, however, suit everybody and whilst the Great Hall, the Doric Arch and the wide sweep of the platforms may have impressed the travelling public, the enthusiast who regarded the railway as a spectator sport tended to be disgruntled by the fact that the place was too spacious to see all that was happening at once. The arrival platforms were a considerable distance from the departure side and the intervening area was a chaos of parcels platforms whose numerous vehicles restricted ones range of vision.

On the other hand many of the trains which served Euston were impressive and would have been out of place in a lesser structure. The terminus served many of the principal northern cities and the better trains that ran to them reflected their importance - few of them, by the 1950s, lacking a title. Gleaming rakes of coaches - sixteen or seventeen in many cases - would be brought into the station by a tank engine, each vehicle being usefully ornamented with a destination board showing the major points of call. Passengers would find their seats, book their meals and, in many cases, pass the last ten minutes or so before departure by wandering down to the business end of the station to watch the engine being attached. Few could fail to be impressed as the ceremony of coupling-up was performed and the locomotive - a mighty Coronation if

one was going to Scotland, or a rebuilt 7P 4-6-0 for most other destinations - prepared for the right away.

Some of the train names were household words and those such as the ROYAL SCOT or the IRISH MAIL were on everybody's lips, having featured often in both serious and popular literature. The second of these was a train of such moment that, until the outbreak of war, a messenger from the foreign office would attend to its departure each evening, presenting the guard with a watch to be taken to Dublin as the Kings Time. The Scots, it is presumed, were judged capable of setting their own timepieces.

Other services, such as the LAKES EXPRESS and the WELSHMAN were more functional than famous, giving an indication of the area served whilst others, such as the COMET, were rather contrived.

We are told, principally by those who have an interest in modern developments and who are too young to remember steam, that one of the points in favour of modernisation was the absence of dirt and grime yet these pictures confirm our older memories of a railway which was much cleaner than it is given credit for; a fact demonstrated in the first of our views which shows an up train decanting its passengers after arriving at

Euston. The date was 15 July 1953, diesels were virtually unknown yet the coaches in the picture, in spite of having run for many hours behind a steam engine, are as clean - cleaner than - anything likely to be seen nowadays.

The second and third photographs depict the best known of Euston's departures - the ROYAL SCOT - getting ready to leave on 31 July 1955 and it is guessed that the reason for the pictures is to secure an early record of the BR maroon livery which had only recently been announced. This may indeed have been their first showing. Porters are much in evidence and the passengers display the British sang-froid reserved - in those days - for public occasions. One did not rush for seats as we do today but, instead, gestured for a porter who could be relied upon to take charge of the baggage and find one's seats. "Smoker, ma'am? Facing the engine, ma'am? Just leave it to me..."

Thus the passengers have time to collect on the platform, marshal their thoughts, say farewells, purchase whatever reading matter is required for the journey and - at the last minute - actually board the train.

Laudable as this self-discipline was, it did have negative effects; the results of which can be discerned on the faces of the two young passengers - now avid BRILL subscribers, no doubt - which show all the frustrations of having been prevented by maternal obstruction from running down to the front end to see which of Staniers masterpieces would be taking then northward.

The final view is of interest since it is an unusual one of Euston, showing the arrangements for the taxicabs and illustrating how easy it was in those days - when it was rather non-U to use the underground - to transfer from train to taxi. How very different from today when it is easier to navigate the escalators and crowds of the tube than to trespass into the black underground cavern to which todays taxi's have been banished.

For more of Old Euston – the latest offering from Irwell Press - **The Great British Railway Station EUSTON. Price £15.95**

Once the pride of the line! Z class (C7) Atlantic 709 turns at Scarborough. Introduced in 1911 - 709 was the second of fifty engines - the Z class shouldered most of the top-link North Eastern traffic until the advent of Pacifics and were probably the company's most celebrated class. Relegated to lighter duties during the Gresley regime, no less than eight were allocated to Scarborough at the end of the last war, remaining until the end of 1949 when the last went to the breakers' yard. *Photograph: N.Stead Coll.*

SCARBOROUGH IN THE THIRTIES 'M B'

The majority of travellers to Scarborough nowadays either use their own cars or ride in one of the many long distance buses and coaches making up the regular traffic jams to be found at peak times on the main A64 road to the coast, from York and the West Riding. Sixty years ago it was very different. Paid holidays for all lay in the future whilst motor cars were reserved mostly for the wealthy

minority. So it was the railway which most people used to reach their hotels and boarding houses.

Scarborough has been in the holiday business for over 150 years. It was a fashionable watering place before the arrival of the railway from York in July 1845, followed two years later by the completion of the line from Hull to Seamer Junction, bringing in even more visitors. The day excursion,

an institution which until recent years provided the reason for many of the visiting trains, first operated into Scarborough a month after the line opened. Tomlinson, in his celebrated "North Eastern Railway History" records the first day excursion in the country running from Newcastle to Scarborough on August 5th 1845. However, there is a contradiction here - it was 1848 before the railway crossed the River Tyne, so a *Newcastle - Scarboro'* train was an impossibility.

As the years went by rail traffic into Scarborough grew, until in the years immediately before World War II it had reached almost un-

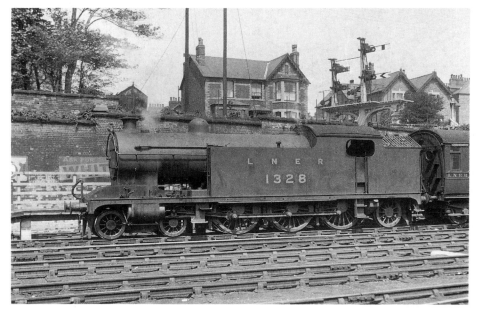

At the time of the photograph, the A8 4-6-2 tanks were something of a local cause celebre, having been rebuilt from the 4-4-4 wheel arrangement to a type more suited to the hilly terrain of the north-east coast. There were forty five engines in the class, many of which handled the passenger services between Darlington and Saltburn and from Middlesbrough to Scarborough. A small number, three to five examples, were allocated to Scarborough and in this view 1328 (later 69891) is seen on empty stock duties at Scarborough. *Photograph Rail Archive Stephenson.*

Probably the most versatile of all the NER main line designs, the B16 4-6-0 was very much a general workhorse of the system and equally at home on goods or express passenger duties. Although not often seen outside the boundaries of the NER, members of the class would occasionally slip through to Kings Cross and one, which found itself 'stranded' at New England in the 1950s was described by a local driver as being 'the best 4-6-0 he had ever handled'. In the above view 1378 (61461 from 1948) takes on water at Scarborough shed. *Photograph Rail Archive Stephenson.*

C6 Atlantic, 701, approaches Scarborough during the 1930s with a load consisting of the ancient and modern - the vehicles next to the engine being of recent design whilst those towards the rear appear somewhat venerable. The C6 class (or Vs as they were prior to the grouping) were the NER's first essay in Atlantics, the first of the class appearing in 1910 as an alternative to 4-6-0 types which had earlier been considered for express duties, although the example shown was one of a second batch, delivered in 1910 with the classification V/09. *Photograph Rail Archive Stephenson.*

A sight which would have delighted pre-war enthusiasts - 2429, a Hull & Barnsley D24 4-4-0, stands at the head of the 18.20 Scarborough - Hull on Wednesday 11 July 1934. *Photograph from the T.E. Rounthwaite collection.*

summer, sixty years ago. I hope readers will find this of interest, as it puts "flesh on the bones" of a public timetable, to conjure up the past.

In 1934 the backbone of the loco fleet were the omnipresent Raven ex-NER B16 class 4-6-0s, all of them at that time in original condition. (Comparative tables for 1959 are included and it was still possible to see up to 25 different members of the class on a typical summer Saturday, though by that year many had been rebuilt and modernised by Gresley and Thompson.)

Assisting the B16s were a number of ex-NER D20 4-4-0s, together with their successors, the Gresley D49s. Incidentally, one of the B16s appearing frequently in 1934 was 925, which came to an untimely end (together with A4 class 4469 - see BRILL 2.5) when York sheds were bombed in 1942.

In 1934 the Gresley V2 was still two years in the future (though they were frequent visitors to Scarboro' in 1959) while the second line of motive power was provided by various Atlantic classes. Prominent amongst these were the ex-GNR class C1 Atlantics, around

manageable proportions. The late Ken Hoole noted that on at least one occasion, evening excursions from Leeds and the West Riding were taking up to four hours to cover the normal one hour journey from York to Scarboro', stopping at every signal due to congestion at the terminus.

Some years ago I acquired the

Train Register Book from Gasworks signalbox (adjacent to Scarboro' loco shed) covering the entire summer of 1934. Entries were meticulously kept, including train reporting numbers and loco numbers. From these it has been possible to reconstruct, with sample tables, a detailed account of the trains to be seen at Scarborough during that

Although the NER opted for the 4-4-2 wheel arrangement - after experimenting with the 4-6-0 type - for its principal services, it produced its final class of 4-4-0s some years afterwards, ten R1s appearing between November 1908 and August 1909; the second of which, 1238, is seen on Scarborough loco during the 1930s. These engines were far from popular, being far heavier on coal than the earlier R class, and their withdrawal was completed at an early date, the last of them disappearing in February 1946. *Photograph Rail Archive Stephenson.*

Table 1

SCARBOROUGH - Whit Monday 21 May 1934
INBOUND (DOWN) TRAFFIC

Time**	Rep No.	From	Loco No.	Class	Notes
08.22		York Parcels	1232	D20 4-4-0	
08.33	X4	Heeley (Sheffield)	722	C7 4-4-2	
08.57	X142	Leeds	849	B16 4-6-0	
09.13	X198	Low Moor (Bradford)	942	B16 4-6-0	
09.18	X27	York	2163	C7 4-4-2	
09.23	X190	Hull	925	B16 4-6-0	
09.39	X75	Murton (Durham)	2196	C7 4-4-2	
09.44	X204	Derby	4643	K2 2-6-0	
09.54	X90		1042	D20 4-4-0	
09.58	X145	Bradford	719	C7 4-4-2	
10.04	X10	Chesterfield	1206	D20 4-4-0	
10.17	X146	Leeds	1929	D17 4-4-0	
10.25		Hull	1207	D20 4-4-0	
10.29	X2	Bradford	2697	J39 0-6-0	
10.34		Pickering	2236 (?)	Railcar	A
10.41	X1	York	2376	B16 4-6-0	
10.45	X183	Hull	1378	B16 4-6-0	
10.53	X178	Horsforth	914	B16 4-6-0	
11.01	X133	Marsden	931	B16 4-6-0	
11.05		Hull	2019	D20 4-4-0	
11.10	X196	Bradford	5052	B6 4-6-0	
11.19		York	2168	C7 4-4-2	
11.35	X112	Newcastle	2200	C7 4-4-2	
11.39	X205	Doncaster	1141	K3 2-6-0	
11.46	X5		728	C7 4-4-2	
11.49	X210	Wigan	2364	B16 4-6-0	
12.12	X248	Leeds	1389	K3 2-6-0	
12.25	X158	Leeds	906	B16 4-6-0	
12.32	X163	Leeds (to Filey)	1382	B16 4-6-0	B
12.36	X27	York	4424	C1 4-4-2	C
13.03	X168	Leeds	1384	B16 4-6-0	
13.08		Pickering	2236(?)	Railcar	A
13.21		Hull	2379	B16 4-6-0	
13.25	X136		924	B16 4-6-0	
13.29	X226	Bradford	3004	J1 0-6-0	
13.34	X32	Bradford	1259	J39 0-6-0	
13.38	X211		1375	B16 4-6-0	
13.50		York	725	D20 4-4-0	
13.53	X195		936	B16 4-6-0	
14.07	X38	Halifax	708	D20 4-4-0	
14.17	X34	Wakefield	1487	J39 0-6-0	
14.20	X244	Bradford	3080	J2 0-6-0	
14.39	X37	Keighley	3071	J2 0-6-0	
14.54	X6	Bolton on Dearne	2368	B16 4-6-0	
15.03	X98		1135	K3 2-6-0	
15.41		Hull	712	D20 4-4-0	
15.46		York	1906	D17 4-4-0	
15.51		Pickering	2236(?)	Railcar	A
17.13		Hull	1537	D22 4-4-0	
17.27	X269	ex Filey	725	D20 4-4-0	D
17.33	X272	Bridlington	1907	D17 4-4-0	
17.58		Pickering	2236(?)	Railcar	
18.07		York	253	D49 4-4-0	
18.59	X270	ex Hunmanby	1906	D17 4-4-0'	D
19.16		York	2371	B16 4-6-0	
19.21		Hull	1051	D20 4-4-0	
19.26	X268	ex Bridlington	1902	D17 4-4-0	
19.39	X163	ex Filey	845	B16 4-6-0	
20.19		Pickering	2236(?)	Railcar	A
20.44		York	4180	D2 4-4-0	

** *Times passing Gasworks signalbox*

A. *Entry refers to 'Pickering Car', probably 2236 BRITISH QUEEN*
B. *Train left for Filey at 13.25 behind B16 845. Note return at 19.39*
C. *Second working of this set which returned to York (D20: 707) after 09.18 arrival*
D. *725 and 1906 light to Filey after arriving in Scarborough at 13.50 and 15.46*

The absence of train descriptions in a number of cases may be explained by the fact that the North Eastern were in the habit of running ad-hoc trains to Scarborough as demand dictated. This was a particular feature of operations at York where an engine and stock would stand in one of the North Bays waiting for whatever traffic presented itself. Neither the driver or guard would know of their destination until the last minute.

twenty different examples being recorded - particularly 4424 and 4447, then stationed at York. Fifteen years later, as 2854 and 2877, they were among the last survivors. York also possessed two of the smaller C2 class, 3984 and 3986, and these were regular visitors to Scarboro'.

NER Atlantics of both C6 and C7 classes appeared daily, but visits by the last batch of twenty C7s (2193 - 2212) were usually restricted to the two regular Scottish holiday trains which came in on Saturdays via Gilling and the double reversal at Malton. These locos, 17 years old, were presumably still on main line express duties between York and Edinburgh.

Two odd ex-NER Atlantics appeared - No.732 (Class C7/2, the rather handsome Gresley rebuild best described as a "stretched D49") and C9 727, ostensibly a 4-4-4 loco with articulated tender.

GCR Atlantics were less common, and restricted to Class C4, no compound C5s appearing. Other GCR passenger locos to show up comprised members of all 4-6-0 types except for B3 "Faringdons" - at that time operating out of Marylebone to Leicester and Sheffield, and the two oldest GC 4-6-0s, Class B1 5195 and 5196, employed on fish trains out of Immingham.

To complete the 4-6-0 section, reference must be made to the other ex-NER types to appear. Out of the twenty 2-cylinder Class B15, fourteen were recorded whilst seven out of the nine surviving operational B13s worked in. I have always had a fascination for the B13, very much a pioneer of its time, following closely on the Highland Railway "Jones Goods" 4-6-0. Both classes disappeared (except for B13 761) by the end of the 1930s. Of the seven B13s, 738 of Hull Dairycoates made the most visits, noted at Scarborough on 17 different days. The others seen that summer, 726, 751, 753, 754, 762 and 775, appeared between one and three times.

Two LNER Standard classes were frequent visitors - the K3 2-6-0s and the prolific J39 0-6-0s, the latter to be found on all types of train, even the occasional outing to and from York on the "Scarboro' Flyer".

Turning now to the smaller

For many years prior to dieselisation and the coincidental tapering off of demand, the volume of traffic at Scarborough during the summer months was so heavy that special arrangements had to be made to relieve the traffic control room at York, (under whose jurisdiction Scarborough came), of much of the additional pressure of seasonal work without causing the control system to lose touch with what was happening. To this end a special one-man control centre was set up in Scarborough signalbox and staffed by a controller from York who would travel daily to the resort. Whilst on duty he would ensure that the resources needed for the days' work were correctly located, amend the booked workings when necessary to meet actual conditions and to keep the parent control at York advised of how matters were developing.

Table 2a		SCARBOROUGH - Saturday 14 July 1934					
Arrivals	Time**	Departures	Rep No.	Engine	Class		Notes
	07.18	07.15 Leeds	305	1907	D17	4-4-0	
	07.43	07.40 Bridlington	308	1206	D20	4-4-0	*
07.10 ex Pickering	07.58		338	505	G5	0-4-4T	
05.50 ex Hull	08.02		342	1051	D20	4-4-0	*
	08.13	08.10 Leeds	300	234	D49	4-4-0	
	08.18	08.15 York (Parcels)	301	2022	D20	4-4-0	
06.40 ex York (Parcels)	08.27		322	1217	D20	4-4-0	
York Goods	08.38			1224	J27	0-6-0	
	08.28	08.25 Hull	307	1470	J39	0-6-0	*
Not recorded	08.44		X19	532	C6	4-4-2	
	08.44	Pickering	338	505	G5	0-4-4T	
	08.58	08.55 Leeds	325	708	D20	4-4-0	
	09.02	Hull Goods		1572	J21	0-6-0	*
Not recorded	09.16		X59	4432	C1	4-4-2	*
Not recorded	09.24		X1	2974	J39	0-6-0	
Not recorded	09.31		X18	2969	J39	0-6-0	
Not recorded	09.45		X30	1375	B16	4-6-0	*
08.50 ex York	09.51		306	1389	K3	2-6-0	
	10.02	10.00 Hull	342	1051	D20	4-4-0	*
08.00 ex Hull	10.05		340	1234	D20	4-4-0	*
08.10 ex Leeds	10.15		351	1243	D21	4-4-0	
	10.19	10.15 York	322	1902	D17	4-4-0	
05.45 ex Deepcar	10.20		354	6020	D9	4-4-0	*
09.05 ex Hull	10.27		348	1380	B16	4-6-0	*
08.55 ex Hull (Q)	10.30		344	842	B16	4-6-0	*
08.45 ex Leeds	10.33		347	1026	D20	4-4-0	
09.47 ex Pickering	10.38		338	505	G5	0-4-4T	
	10.40	10.35 Leeds	306	532	C6	4-4-2	
09.40 ex York	10.44		323	727	C9	4-4-2	
(Scarborough Flyer)	11.03	11.00 Kings Cross	312	2969	J39	0-6-0	
	11.08	11.05 Leeds	351	1217	D20	4-4-0	
09.00 ex Normanton	11.08		321	255	D49	4-4-0	
	11.12	11.10 Hull	340	845	B16	4-6-0	*
09.15 ex Leeds	11.15		349	848	B16	4-6-0	
	11.19	Pickering	338	505	G5	0-4-4T	
	11.23	11.20 Glasgow	309	728	C7	4-4-2	
09.45 ex Hull	11.26		341	942	B16	4-6-0	*
10.10 ex Leeds (Non-stop)	11.32		350	220	D49	4-4-0	
	11.36	11.35 York	Spl	1375	B16	4-6-0	
Not recorded	11.44		X25	247	D49	4-4-0	
Not recorded	11.49		X22	707	D20	4-4-0	
07.59 ex Low Moor	11.53		357	4463	LMS 4F	0-6-0	*
	12.02	12.00 Kings Cross	302	4413	C1	4-4-2	*
Not recorded	12.03		X17	1906	D17	4-4-0	
08.10 ex Heeley	12.22		352	815	B15	4-6-0	
	12.25	Excn to Filey	X17	34	J21	0-6-0	
Not recorded	12.28		X61	1298	J39	0-6-0	
	12.37	12.20 Leeds	348	1480	J39	0-6-0	
	12.38	12.25 Leicester (GC)	354	4432	C1	4-4-2	
10.45 ex Hull	12.41		346	930	B16	4-6-0	
	12.44	12.40 Liverpool (Cen)	311	727	C9	4-4-2	
07.55 ex Liverpool (Cen)	12.45		328	5427	B2	4-6-0	
08.23 ex Derby (Mid)	12.51		359	823	B15	4-6-0	
Not recorded	13.00		X28	1397	K3	2-6-0	
12.15 ex Pickering	13.11		338	505	G5	0-4-4T	
11.05 ex Hull	13.15		308	1470	J39	0-6-0	
	13.17	13.15 Leeds	321	1243	D21	4-4-0	
Not recorded	13.19		X29	844	B16	4-6-0	
Not recorded	13.23		X16	1376	B16	4-6-0	

Via Filey route. **Times passing Gasworks signalbox. *Q Runs when required.*

In their heyday between being introduced in 1896 and being superseded by the R class of 4-4-0's at the turn of the century, the Q class handled much of the express traffic between Newcastle and Edinburgh. After this relatively brief spell in the limelight they were relegated to lighter work between Newcastle and Leeds or York and in this view 1907 (redesignated D17/2 by the LNER) stands on Scarborough shed, in the company of a GN 4-4-2, after having arrived with the 13.15 ex Hull. Photograph by the late T.E. Rounthwaite.

passenger locos, various 4-4-0s were observed. D20 and D49 have been mentioned already, and earlier varieties of ex-NER 4-4-0 were also seen. Both types of D17 (NER classes M and Q) were common, and a last glimpse of a small Worsdell came on Whit Monday - see table - when 1537, a D22, made what was probably its final bow. Another 4-4-0 class to vanish in 1934 was the ex-Hull and Barnsley D24. Of the five built, only 2429 lasted through the summer of 1934. Stored at Springhead, it was returned to traffic at the start of the peak summer timetable and from July 9th made a daily appearance at 6.20pm on a fast return working. However, ten days of this activity was obviously enough for it and it never reappeared in Scarborough after July 20th, being subsequently photographed in September 1934 at Darlington, for scrap.

Other 4-4-0s were of GCR origin, with examples of both Director classes - D10 5431 and 5437 and D11 Nos.5501, 5509 and 5511 recorded, along with several of the earlier class D9. Finally a handful of ex-GNR D2 and D3 types appeared when power was short - examples of both types resided at York and Hull.

The aristocratic lines of the NER 4-4-0 at seen at their best in R class 708 as it stands on Scarborough shed. These engines were introduced in 1899 as the principal express passenger class of the North Eastern and, although superseded by atlantics from 1903, continued in front-line service until ousted by the influx of Gresley Pacifics. In their later years the class was to be found on most secondary routes of the NER and most survived to be taken into BR stock in 1948. The last survivor of the class was to be found working between Alnmouth and Alnwick as recently as November 1957. *Photograph Rail Archive Stephenson.*

Table 2b — SCARBOROUGH - Saturday 14 July 1934

Arrivals	Time**	Departures	Rep No.	Engine	Class	Notes
	13.30	Pickering local	338	505	G5 0-4-4T	
08.55 ex Manchester (Vic)	13.34		300	4216	LMS 4F 0-6-0	
Add'l ex York	13.39			1232	D20 4-4-0	
09.50 ex Manchester (Vic)	13.44		301	1907	D17 4-4-0	
11.55 ex Leeds	13.51		325	1238	D21 4-4-0	
08.25 ex Leicester (MR)	13.57		302	2376	B16 4-6-0	*
	13.59	13.45 Manchester (Vic)	301	4463	LMS 4F 0-6-0	
09.30 ex Birmingham	14.02		326	775	B13 4-6-0	
	14.04	14.00 Bradford	349	220	D49 4-4-0	
	14.10	14.05 Heeley	352	942	B16 4-6-0	*
	14.13	13.55 Leicester (GC)	303	255	D49 4-4-0	
	14.16	14.10 Hull	346	1234	D20 4-4-0	*
12.50 ex York	14.16		305	708	D20 4-4-0	
Not recorded	14.28		X121	924	B16 4-6-0	
12.50 ex Hull	14.35		343	1206	D20 4-4-0	*
	14.38	14.27 Leeds	347	848	B16 4-6-0	
	14.40	14.35 Glasgow	315	707	D20 4-4-0	
	14.43	14.20 Hull	308	930	B16 4-6-0	*
10.00 ex Blackburn	14.57		358	782	B15 4-6-0	*
12.56 ex Leeds	15.03		306	234	D49 4-4-0	
	15.03	14.45 Manchester	300	1298	J39 0-6-0	
	15.13	Not recorded	X13	1380	B16 4-6-0	
12.00 ex Newcastle	15.13		322	2022	D20 4-4-0	
	15.26	15.10 Manchester (L.R)	328	5427	B2 4-6-0	
10.10 ex Kings Cross	15.27		327	1902	D17 4-4-0	
	15.29	15.00 Kings Norton	326	1907	D17 4-4-0	
10.35 ex Liverpool	15.31		330	232	D49 4-4-0	
	15.36	15.20 Leicester (MR)	302	842	B16 4-6-0	*
13.00 ex Hull	15.40		342	2429	D24 4-4-0	*
Not recorded	15.47		X11	2368	B16 4-6-0	
Pickering local	15.50		338	505	G5 0-4-4T	
13.20 ex Bradford	15.54		312	1240	D21 4-4-0	
	15.56	15.45 Leeds	305	1470	J39 0-6-0	
	16.06	16.05 Blackburn	358	4216	LMS 4F 0-6-0	*
Scarborough Flyer	16.07		329	2969	J39 0-6-0	
	16.16	Pickering local	338	505	G5 0-4-4T	
15.30 ex York	16.23		321	2017	D20 4-4-0	
	16.26	Not recorded	X20	234	D49 4-4-0	
14.00 ex Leeds	16.30		351	1244	D21 4-4-0	
	16.31	16.27 Hull	343	708	D20 4-4-0	*
	16.44	16.40 Leeds	325	1238	D21 4-4-0	
	16.49	16.45 Derby (MR)	359	823	B15 4-6-0	*
15.03 ex Hull	16.52		345	726	B13 4-6-0	*
	16.56	16.50 Leeds	351	232	D49 4-4-0	
15.15 ex Hull	17.00		340	1051	D20 4-4-0	*
08.25 ex Leicester (GC)	17.10		360	2474	J23 0-6-0	* A
	17.18	17.15 Hull	342	1026	D20 4-4-0	*
10.30 ex Edinburgh	17.24		310	2208	C7 4-4-2	
	17.31	17.10 Newcastle	322	1232	D20 4-4-0	
	17.40	York Goods		1224	J27 0-6-0	
17.05 ex York	17.52		303	1378	B16 4-6-0	
Pickering local	18.03		338	505	G5 0-4-4T	
	18.07	18.05 Leeds	312	1244	D21 4-4-0	
16.42 ex Leeds	18.08		300	211	D49 4-4-0	
	18.22	18.20 Hull	345	2429	D24 4-4-0	*
	18.27	Pickering local	338	505	G5 0-4-4T	
17.08 ex Hull	18.31		307	2019	D20 4-4-0	*
	18.34	X25 empty stock		247	D49 4-4-0	
	18.39	18.35 Hull	340	726	B13 4-6-0	*

* Via Filey route.   ** Times passing Gasworks signalbox

A. 360 arrived 230 minutes late, probably due to engine failure. 2474 had been carriage pilot all day until disappearing at about 16.15, presumably summoned to rescue 360 which must have been stranded near Filey.

Although the season of 1934, described in this article, was busy the previous year had been chaotic - because of an increase in traffic and the poor layout of the trackwork around Scarborough station - and costly enhancements were made early in the year in order to improve the working of trains.

One of the major difficulties concerned the working of trains to the Whitby area which invariably started from the up side of the station, crossed - thus blocking - all lines to get to the down side where the engine rounded its train before reversing direction. The result was to obstruct either all or part of the main lines for several minutes at a time when approaching trains were occupying every block section for miles back.

The solution reached was to create a new platform on the down side of Scarborough station, achieved by extending platform 1 and using the outer face as platform 1a, from which Whitby trains could be propelled the short distance to Londesborough Road where they reversed without any need to run-round the train. In addition to resolving the problem of the Whitby reversals, the extension of platform 1 allowed trains of more than fourteen vehicles to use the Central station - the limit had previously been thirteen - as well as Londesborough Road.

At first sight a visit by a GN Atlantic to Scarborough; an interesting although by no means unknown occurrence since after the grouping a small number were allocated to York and were used when occasion demanded for additional work to Scarborough. On closer examination, however, 4447 - one of the York allocation - has a number of subtle alterations distinguishing it from the remainder of the class - modifications made in 1923 when its chimney and cab roof were altered to allow it to take part in main line tests between Newcastle and Edinburgh. *Photograph Rail Archive Stephenson.*

Although an LNER design, the Gresley D49 class were seldom, if ever, seen south of Doncaster and, for southerners, a long pilgrimage was necessary to catch sight of them. Inside NER territory, however, the 76-strong class was common enough, one of their especial tasks being the haulage of many of the through Leeds - Scarborough services until displaced by diesel multiple-units in the late 1950s. In this view a well cleaned 322 (later 62722) HUNTINGDONSHIRE waits for its next turn of duty at Scarborough. *Photograph N. Stead Coll.*

| Table 2c | | SCARBOROUGH - Saturday 14 July 1934 (Continued) | | | | |
Arrivals	Time**	Departures	Rep No.	Engine	Class	Notes
	19.02	19.00 Leeds	300	2017	D20 4-4-0	
	19.11	Not recorded	X19	2969	J39 0-6-0	
13.40 ex Kings Cross	19.14		302	4413	C1 4-4-2	*
	19.18	19.15 Deepcar	360	1147	D20 4-4-0	A *
17.30 ex Leeds	19.19		305	1375	B16 4-6-0	
	19.30	X19 empty stock		2208	C7 4-4-2	
	19.44	19.40 Hull	341	1376	B16 4-6-0	*
12.40 ex Glasgow	19.46		309	716	C7 4-4-2	
18.05 ex Hull	19.51		308	845	B16 4-6-0	*
	20.00	19.55 Leeds	323	1240	D21 4-4-0	
Ex Filey	20.01		X17	34	J21 0-6-0	*
19.15 ex York	20.12		311	707	D20 4-4-0	
	20.13	20.05 Leeds (Mail)	307	211	D49 4-4-0	
Pickering local	20.17		338	505	G5 0-4-4T	
	20.22	Not recorded	X17	775	B13 4-6-0	
	20.34	20.30 Hull	308	2019	D20 4-4-0	*
19.05 ex Hull	20.34		343	708	D20 4-4-0	*
	20.39	Not recorded	X1	2974	J39 0-6-0	
	20.46	Not recorded	X11	2368	B16 4-6-0	
	20.51	Pickering local	338	505	G5 0-4-4T	
	21.03	21.00 Hull	344	1051	D20 4-4-0	*
	21.07	Not recorded	X29	844	B16 4-6-0	
19.25 ex Leeds	21.19		325	1217	D20 4-4-0	
	21.26	Not recorded	X28	1397	J39 0-6-0	
	21.36	Not recorded	X121	924	B16 4-6-0	
	21.40	Not recorded	X30	782	B15 4-6-0	*
	21.52	309 empty stock		716	C7 4-4-2	
	22.00	21.55 Hull	343	2376	B16 4-6-0	*
	22.05	22.00 York	311	1907	D17 4-4-0	
	22.13	Not recorded	X59	1375	B16 4-6-0	*
20.45 ex Leeds	22.16		312	1470	J39 0-6-0	

A 6020 (D9) as pilot.   * Via Filey route.   ** Times passing Gasworks signalbox.

Scarborough, though an exceptionally busy station in the summer, did not enjoy an especially high status as a motive power location and, indeed, its allocation of locomotives - usually just over a dozen engines - gave no clues whatever to the volume of traffic using the station, most of which was worked by foreign engines and men.

The responsibilities of the shed, 50E, lay not so much with the visiting excursion traffic (apart from the working of empty stock from the sidings to the station and vice versa) as with the workaday locals along the Yorkshire coast to Whitby and the minor NER expresses to York and Leeds (City). For the former the shed had a batch of about five A8 4-6-2 tanks whilst the faster trains on the Malton road were given Gresley D49 4-4-0s - the usual allocation at Scarborough being four of the class. In addition about three other 0-6-0 engines were provided to deal with shunting and station pilot duties. A surprising member of the Scarborough allocation was an LMS Ivatt 4MT 2-6-0, 43052, sent there as a replacement for a B16 4-6-0, shortly after nationalisation; one of a number of the class that the NER, rather curiously, managed to acquire - several other examples being allocated to Selby.

In spite of the widespread dieselisation by multiple units on the NER - about 1958 and considerably earlier than the rest of the system - and the fact that many local lines ceased operations at about the same time, Scarborough's steam allocation remained surprisingly static (albeit without much work to do) until the early 1960s by which time sufficient units and diesel locomotives had been delivered to allow the shed to close; it lost its allocation in March 1963.

In contrast to the classic lines of some of its 4-4-0 and Atlantic locomotives, is the rather stark - if not ugly - shape of the NER B13 4-6-0. Introduced in 1899, just ahead of the Atlantic 'revolution', the B13s spent very little time on top-link workings but found useful employment on a variety of secondary duties, notably fish between Hull and Doncaster. 738 is at the latter place in May 1937, a year before its withdrawal and eighteen months prior to the extinction of the class. They were regular visitors to Scarborough during the summer months. *Photograph N. Stead Coll.*

Arrivals	Arrive	Depart	Departures	Rep No.	Engine	Class	Pilot	Notes
			SCARBOROUGH - Saturday 18 July 1959					
04.30 ex York	05.29				61240	B1 4-6-0		
23.20 ex Glasgow	06.07			125	61440	B16 4-6-0		
Relief ex Glasgow	06.22			444	61943	K3 2-6-0	61438 (B16)	
		06.45	Filey HC	304	82026	BR3 2-6-2T		*
		07.02	Filey ECS	308	61440	B16 4-6-0		*
05.35 ex Hull	07.09			606	DMU			*
York Parcels	07.16	07.10	Leeds	301	61240	B1 4-6-0		
				327	42764	LM2-6-0	61069 (B1)	
		07.23	Hull	317	DMU			*
		07.58	Filey ECS	309	61438	B16 4-6-0		*
		08.07	Leeds	306	61943	K3 2-6-0		
07.53 Filey - Glasgow	08.10			304	82026	BR3 2-6-2T		*
York Parcels	08.15			322	61229	B1 4-6-0		
		08.15	Hull	312	61893	K3 2-6-0		*
		08.20	Glasgow	304	61069	B1 4-6-0		
		08.28	Hull	606	DMU			*
		08.34	Filey HC ECS	183	42764	LM 2-6-0		*
		08.40	Glasgow	313	60947	V2 2-6-2		
		09.00	Filey HC ECS	307	61435	B16 4-6-0		*
		09.08	Newcastle	310	60887	V2 2-6-2		
07.38 ex Hull	09.26			604	DMU			*
		09.29	Manchester (Ex)	314	61305	B1 4-6-0		
		09.40	Leicester (MR)	289	61467	B16 4-6-0		
06.15 ex Grantham	09.44			301	61452	B16 4-6-0		
08.12 ex Leeds	09.55			341	61447	B16 4-6-0		
		09.55	Leeds	305	61068	B1 4-6-0		
		10.00	Manchester (LR)	187	61437	B16 4-6-0		*
09.10 ex York	10.04			318	73161	BR5 4-6-0		
		10.05	Leeds	322	61424	B16 4-6-0		
		10.25	Glasgow	302	60924	V2 2-6-2		
08.55 ex Leeds	10.25			342	61446	B16 4-6-0		
09.00 ex Hull	10.32			603	62720	D49 4-4-0	62710 (D49)	
08.50 ex Normanton	10.37			319	61450	B16 4-6-0	61420 (B16)	
(The Scarborough Flyer)		10.42	Kings Cross	311	61229	B1 4-6-0		
		10.50	Newcastle	303	61475	B16 4-6-0		
		11.00	Filey	327	DMU			*
08.18 ex Sheffield (GC)	11.01			188	61453	B16 4-6-0		
		11.05	Bradford (MR)	342	61016	B1 4-6-0		
07.55 ex Sheffield (MR)	11.07			286	61457	B16 4-6-0		*
08.42 ex Bradford (MR)	11.14			323	73160	BR5 4-6-0		
		11.15	Hull	604	DMU			*
Relief ex Stalybridge	11.20			W614	45075	LM5 4-6-0		
		11.25	Liverpool (Ex)	238	43098	LM4 2-6-0	62770 (D49)	
		11.30	Hull	603	61306	B1 4-6-0		*
10.00 ex Leeds	11.32			321	61472	B16 4-6-0		
08.27 ex Derby	11.42	11.35	Derby	299	73161	BR5 4-6-0		
				290	60948	V2 2-6-2		
10.05 ex Hull	11.47	11.45	Manchester (Vic)	242	61452	B16 4-6-2		
				614	DMU			*
09.35 ex Sheffield (GC)	11.53	11.50	Leicester (GC)	193	61469	B16 4-6-0		*
				194	61334	B1 4-6-0		
08.50 ex Manchester (Vic)	12.16	12.15	Kings Norton	300	61450	B16 4-6-0		
10.40 ex Hull	12.21			231	61194	B1 4-6-0		
				349	DMU			*
Preston add'l	12.26	12.25	Sowerby Bridge	228	61420	B16 4-6-0		*
				C860	61429	B16 4-6-0		
08.20 ex Chesterfield (MR)	12.32			288	44265	LM4 0-6-0		*
		12.38	York	319	73160	BR5 4-6-0		
08.25 ex Leicester (MR)	12.40			296	44336	BR4 0-6-0		
08.30 Mancheser (Vic)	12.45			247	61471	B16 4-6-0		*
		12.50	Hull	614	DMU			*

* Via Filey route. Note. Arr/Dep times are as per WTT/STN and not the actual times.

Returning to the subject of ex-H&B locos, 1934 found a number of J23 and J28 0-6-0s still active, and several made the journey to Scarborough that summer. On July 4th two day excursions - probably a school outing, ran from Pickering behind J23s 2453 and 2455, both from Malton shed. J23 2474 was employed as Scarborough station pilot from time to time and on July 14th (see table) found itself on front line duty. J28 2408 appeared on August 11th on the 3.15pm from Hull (running 50 minutes late) and returned south on the 9.20pm, whilst J23s 2444, 2452 and 2454 came in on odd occasions from Pickering. However, undoubtedly the star attraction of this section was an excursion on August 26th behind a domeless or "straightback" J23, 2464, a rare sight by the mid-thirties.

Several pre-grouping 0-6-0 types appeared, including ex-GNR J1, J2 and J6, several ex-GCR J11s and, mostly on goods turns, ex-NER J21, J24 and J25 classes, whilst the Hull goods often produced a J26 and the York goods *always* produced a J27. Incidentally, both J21 876 and J27 2392 (now preserved) were numbered amongst the visitors. Another pre-grouping class often to be seen on excursion traffic was the ex-GNR K2 2-6-0.

The Pickering - Scarborough service, rostered for Sentinel Railcar 2236 BRITISH QUEEN frequently produced a loco plus coach as the Sentinels were somewhat unreliable. G5 505 was a frequent performer, but on odd occasions an ex-NER or ex-HBR 0-6-0 would appear, whilst for several days in early September one of the last surviving ex-NER 2-4-2Ts, class F8 1581, was on the working.

To close the narrative, mention must be made of a solitary visit by an LMS Crab 2844, on June 30th - other LMS locos to turn up were invariably Fowler 4F 0-6-0s - and

Train for Manchester — Scarborough (Londesboro' Road) B16 No.61454 in charge. *Photograph K. Hoole N.Stead Coll.*

Arrivals	Arr	Dep	Departures	Rep No.	Engine	Class	Pilot
		13.00	Glasgow	301	61453	B16 4-6-0	
07.45 ex Hertford North	13.05	13.05		311	61337	B1 4-6-0	
		13.10	Manchester (Vic)	341	61446	B16 4-6-0	
		13.15	Halifax	211	45075	LM5 4-6-0	
08.20 ex Kings Norton	13.20			298	60975	V2 2-6-2	
08.25 ex Leicester (GC)	13.25			22	61122	B1 4-6-0	*
09.35 ex Sowerby Bridge	13.33			233	43123	LM4 2-6-0	62740 (D49) *
Relief ex Glasgow	13.38			434	61456	B16 4-6-0	
08.05 Blackburn-Filey ECS	13.50			223	61941	K3 2-6-0	*
		13.55	Blackburn	224	61194	B1 4-6-0	*
12.16 ex Leeds	13.56			305	61925	K3 2-6-0	
		14.00	Sheffield (GC)	195	61334	B1 4-6-0	
09.17 ex Basford North	14.02			10	61803	K3 2-6-0	*
Relief ex Edinburgh	14.07			435	61185	B1 4-6-0	
		14.10	Kings Cross	321	60948	V2 2-6-2	
10.45 ex Newcastle	14.12			302	61353	B1 4-6-0	
12.45 ex Hull	14.26			317	61922	K3 2-6-0	*
		14.30	Sheffield (MR)	309	44265	LM4 0-6-0	
Relief ex Glasgow	14.31			436	61229	B1 4-6-0	
		14.35	Basford North	209	44336	LM4 0-6-0	*
12.42 ex Leeds	14.37			322	61305	B1 4-6-0	
		14.40	Doncaster ECS (434)	476	61471	B16 4-6-0	
09.05 ex Liverpool (Ex)	14.42			239	61466	B16 4-6-0	
09.55 ex Manchester (LR)	14.50			200	61181	B1 4-6-0	
08.05 ex Glasgow	14.55			304	61259	B1 4-6-0	
		14.55	Hull	349	DMU		*
		15.00	Cherry Tree	C862	42845	LM 2-6-0	*
		15.05	York ECS(22)	223	61472	B16 4-6-0	
		15.12	Doncaster ECS (10)	477	62720	D49 4-4-0	
		15.20	York	322	61434	B16 4-6-0	
13.08 ex Bradford (MR)	15.26			324	80120	BR4 2-6-4T	
		15.35	Doncaster ECS (436)	478	61166	B1 4-6-0	
10.28 ex Kings Cross	15.42			326	61276	B1 4-6-0	
14.10 ex Hull	15.47			604	DMU		*
14.10 ex Leeds	15.52			342	61068	B1 4-6-0	
		16.00	Leeds	305	62710	D49 4-4-0	
11.28 ex Kings Cross	16.11			320	73161	BR5 4-6-0	
		16.15	Bradford	323	61447	B16 4-6-0	
Relief ex Singer (Glasgow)	16.21			438	61452	B16 4-6-0	
		16.25	Starbeck ECS	228	61456	B16 4-6-0	
		16.30	Hull	317	61922	K3 2-6-0	*
		16.38	York (Parcels)	315	61259	B1 4-6-0	
09.20 ex Glasgow	16.40			303	61069	B1 4-6-0	
		17.10	York ECS (305)	224	61229	B1 4-6-0	
15.45 ex Hull	17.17			614	DMU		*
		17.30	Swindon	188	61305	B1 4-6-0	
16.45 ex York	17.45	17.40	Doncaster ECS (438)	479	60975	V2 2-6-2	
Relief ex Glasgow	17.55			319	61071	B1 4-6-0	
				451	61084	B1 4-6-0	
		17.55	Leeds	324	80120	BR4 2-6-4T	
		18.00	Hull	604	DMU		*
16.25 ex Leeds	18.08			314	61062	B1 4-6-0	
		18.24	Hull	614	DMU		*
		18.30	Doncaster	318	61122	B1 4-6-0	
				452	61435	B16 4-6-0	
Relief ex Glasgow	18.58	19.30	Normanton	311	61337	B1 4-6-0	
		19.40	Leeds	342	61062	B1 4-6-0	
17.43 ex Leeds	19.40			306	61434	B16 4-6-0	
17.45 ex Hull	19.45			606	DMU		*
		20.00	York	319	61276	B1 4-6-0	
		20.25	Hull	606	DMU		*
		20.35	Doncaster ECS (451)	480	61181	B1 4-6-0	
		20.45	York ECS (200)	225	61071	B1 4-6-0	
		20.55	York ECS (342)	226	61452	B16 4-6-0	
		21.15	York	316	61434	B16 4-6-0	
		21.25	York ECS (303)	227	61084	B1 4-6-0	
20.30 ex York	21.31			315	61467	B16 4-6-0	
		21.35	Doncaster ECS (452)	481	61435	B16 4-6-0	
		21.55	Selby ECS (298)	229	61466	B16 4-6-0	

Station pilots : 62739 and 62762 (D49 4-4-0)

* Via Filey route. NB 18 July was the start of the Glasgow holidays. Note. Arr/Dep times as per WTT/STN.

an appearance by the last single wheeler on the LNER, X2 2-2-4T 957 based at Hull Botanic Gardens, which hauled the inspection saloon into Scarborough on July 17th, possibly in connection with the annual station gardens competition. Finally, a mystery. August 23rd contains an entry for an ecs into Scarborough behind loco 5960, which returned west light engine. Now the number is quoted twice, clearly. It could not have been the ex-LNWR Claughton as LMS 5960 was withdrawn in March 1934. LNER 5960 was an ex-GCR Q4 0-8-0, a type unknown on coaching stock duties. It has been suggested the loco might have been 5950 or 5980, both J11s, but the problem remains unsolved.

Turning briefly to the comparative 1959 list, this is typical of the number and type of trains and locos to appear in what was the last year before the onset of dieselisation. As remarked earlier, B16s were still much in evidence, although at the end of their days, but the most interesting feature to note is that twenty five years on from the hectic mid-thirties, the number of trains had not dropped significantly. Contrast that with today, when excursions rarely appear, and the long distance holiday trains have but one survivor, the through HST from Glasgow which still ran on peak Saturdays in 1993. At the time of writing it is not known if this will occur again in 1994. It is sincerely hoped this will be the case, forming a last echo of interesting days long past.

Under Gresley many NER secondary duties remained powered by North Eastern locomotives and it was not until the arrival of the Thompson B1 4-6-0s after the war that the ranks of the pre-grouping engines started to seriously thin. In this view 61198 of Darlington - probably quite a stranger to the area - passes Londesborough Road en route to Scarborough in the mid-fifties with an excursion from the York direction.
Photograph K.Hoole N.Stead Coll.

THE THANET BELLE

by D.W. Winkworth

Shortly before being ousted by BR 5MT 4-6-0s, a well cleaned N15, 30768 SIR BALIN, runs into Margate with the Ramsgate-bound Kentish Belle in August 1955. *Photograph by arrangement John Tatchell.*

After the Second World War the Southern Railway authorities were determined to restore passenger services to normal as soon as possible and to introduce a couple of new all-Pullman trains, one to the West Country and the other to Kent.

The initial proposal, so far as Kent was concerned, put forward on 27th May 1946, was for a service to leave London Victoria at 10.20am, call at Margate and Broadstairs and arrive at Ramsgate at 12.10pm, with a return train from Ramsgate at either 5.10pm or 6.10pm, also taking 100 minutes. At a meeting between the SR and the Pullman Car Company in September, it was proposed that the train should be introduced for the summer of 1947, using seven third class and three first class Pullman cars, on a return circuit leaving Victoria in the morning and going via Margate, Broadstairs, Ramsgate and Folkestone to London Charing Cross and then, in the afternoon, retracing its way to Folkestone, Ramsgate and Victoria.

On 10th February 1947 the SR traffic manager outlined his proposals in some detail to his general manager; the proposed daily timings being shown in table 1.

The Pullman cars proposed to form

In the early days of the Pullman, an unrebuilt West Country light Pacific wheels the Thanet Belle through the Kentish countryside. For most of the year, when the train consisted of both Pullman and conventional stock, the usual engine was a King Arthur 4-6-0 or, after 1955, a BR standard 5MT. In the summer, however, when the train ran as an all-Pullman service, a Pacific was very often to be found on the working. *Photograph D.W. Winkworth.*

Table 1. PROPOSED TIMINGS	
LONDON (Victoria)	10.10
Whitstable	11.31
Herne Bay	11.40
Margate	11.48
RAMSGATE (arr)	12.10
RAMSGATE (dep)	13.00
Sandwich	13.15
Deal	13.25
Walmer	13.30
Martin Mill	13.38
Dover (Priory)	13.52
Folkestone (Central)	14.07
LONDON (Waterloo)	15.26
LONDON (Charing Cross) arr	15.30
LONDON (Charing Cross) dep	16.15
LONDON (Waterloo)	16.18
Folkestone (Central)	17.40
Dover (Priory)	17.15
Martin Mill	18.09
Walmer	18.14
Deal	18.19
Sandwich	18.28
RAMSGATE (arr)	18.43
RAMSGATE (dep)	19.00
Margate	19.20
Herne Bay	19.38
Whitstable	19.47
LONDON (Victoria)	21.05

the train were all of 1921/2 vintage; Nos 11, 15, 16 and 30 (a picnic car with kitchen) were third class vehicles and CORAL, ELMIRA, ERMINIE, MAID OF KENT, FORMOSA and ANACONDA composite class cars. ELMIRA, ERMINIE and ANACONDA had all suffered some damage by enemy action and, because the PCC was fully occupied in preparing cars for the DEVON BELLE, attention could not be given to those three for some while. The question was also raised as to what type of train would be required when electrification (in theory expected in the early 1950s) was introduced; would it be electric multiple units, or would Pullman stock be locomotive hauled (electric, steam or diesel-electric?)

The following day the traffic manager advised the general manager that he proposed to defer the introduction of the KENTISH BELLE. Elliot, the deputy general manager, got to know about this and called for a analysis of the stock position. On 14th February a memorandum reached him to the effect that there were available and ready for use six composite cars and four third class Pullmans, with the added comment "In view of the shortage of passenger rolling stock it is difficult to see why an all-Pullman train

		SX	SO
LONDON (Victoria)	dep	11.30	15.05
Whitstable	dep	12.52	16.30
Herne Bay	dep	13.01	16.39
Margate	dep	13.17	16.56
Broadstairs	dep	13.28	17.07
RAMSGATE	arr	13.34	17.15
		SSX	SSO
RAMSGATE	dep	17.05	18.15
Broadstairs	dep	17.10	18.20
Margate	dep	17.18	18.29
Herne Bay	dep	17.35	18.48
Whitstable	dep	17.44	18.57
LONDON (Victoria)	arr	19.10	20.20

Notes
SX : Saturdays excepted
SO : Saturdays only
SSX: Saturdays and Sundays excepted
SSO: Saturdays and Sundays only

should not run". Also put forward was another schedule, this one starting at Charing Cross at about 10.15am to Folkestone and Ramsgate, continuing from there around midday to Victoria and returning in the afternoon to Ramsgate and on round to Folkestone and Charing Cross in the evening. Despite this, the traffic manager got his way when he was informed by the general manager on 24th February that introduction of the train would be deferred as suggested.

A doubly apposite photograph showing the subject of the article at a location where one of the Irwell ensemble spent several years as stationmaster. An unkempt and unidentified Schools 4-4-0 raises a head of steam whilst standing at Herne Bay prior to attacking the steep gradient on Blacksole bank with the 11.35 Victoria - Ramsgate. Although at the time of the picture, autumn 1958, steam traction was unchallenged in East Kent, the newly laid, and as yet unenergised, third rail suggests the changes that were to take place from June 1959. *Photograph D.W. Winkworth*

Every inch a train. The 11.15 (SO) Kentish Belle from Ramsgate nears the end of its trip to Victoria on 27 July 1957, passing Shortlands Junction behind N15 4-6-0 30806 SIR GALLERON of Hither Green; an engine not normally seen on ex-LCDR metals. It is a pity that the classic lines depicted in the photograph could not have been completed by the inclusion of the headboard. *Photograph R.C. Riley.*

A light Pacific working the evening up service not long after the trains introduction. Contrasting with the apparent modernity of the Bulleid locomotive - and the opulence of the Pullman cars - is a rather venerable-looking multiple-unit working a Victoria outer-suburban service. *Photograph D.W. Winkworth.*

74

Elegant and opulent. In a time when multiple-units rule the day - as they have on the ex-LCDR since 1959 - it is difficult to believe that anything as exceptional as a Pullman car could have been used quite ordinarily between London and the Kent coast resorts. In this view Pullman brake-third No.16 pauses at Ramsgate between duties. The extent to which these vehicles had to shine beggars belief and not only were the interiors pristine but the exteriors had to be srubbed and polished until they became mirror-like. One former Ramsgate carriage cleaner relates that even the handrails came under the closest scrutiny and that not even the slightest blemish escaped the Inspectors careful eye. Matters were not helped by the fact that one of the most senior of the Pullman management - a fiery character - lived at Birchington and made a habit of strolling down to the station to perform his own ad-hoc inspections. *Photograph N.C.Simmons*

Consequently the matter remained dormant for about a year; nationalisation took place in the meantime and John Elliot became chief regional officer (equivalent, in broad terms, to general manager). The operating and commercial departments reported to him that a Saturday service could be - Victoria depart 3.5pm, calling at Whitstable (4.30pm), Herne Bay (4.39pm), Margate (4.57pm) Broadstairs (5.8pm) with an arrival at Ramsgate at 5.15pm. The return would be made from Ramsgate, by the same route, at 6.15pm. Otherwise the service should be 10.10am from Victoria to Ramsgate, 1pm Ramsgate to Charing Cross, 4.15pm Charing Cross to Ramsgate with the final leg from Ramsgate at 7pm for Victoria. However, by the beginning of March, Elliot had decided that the train, to be known as the THANET BELLE (the terms Thanet and Kentish were virtually interchangeable until this point, possibly because of the likelihood of serving Folkestone), would operate between London Victoria and Ramsgate via Herne Bay each way.

Accordingly, the THANET BELLE entered the timetable on a summer only basis, with the timings reproduced in table 2.

The inaugural train ran on 31st

May 1948, made up of ten Pullmans (first class cars CORAL and FORMOSA and third class cars 11, 15, 16, 96, 132, 133, 135 and 137) which provided for 44 first and 225 third - class passengers. The Pullman Car Com-

pany had been busy in refurbishing the cars; Nos 11, 15 and 16 had been converted to brake parlour cars, No. 96 - the only twelve-wheeler in the set - had previously been SYLVIA, and Nos 132, 133, 135 and 137 (ANACONDA,

The up afternoon Kentish Belle approaches Bromley South behind an unrebuilt West Country 4-6-2 during the mid-fifties. *Photograph D.W. Winkworth.*

No problem! In spite of the 1 in 96 climb, N15 30767 SIR VALENCE has a clean exhaust and even a surplus of steam as it hauls the 11.35 'Belle' up the bank towards Bickley on Sunday 5 August 1957. *Photograph R.C.Riley.*

ERMINIE, ELMIRA and MAID OF KENT respectively) were all down-graded from composite to third class. Later on FORMOSA was renamed MAID OF KENT. Supplementary fees of 3s 6d first-class and two shillings third class one way were charged.

The engine used for the first service was Battle of Britain class 4-6-2 No. 21C170 MANSTON; this Royal Air Force station was, of course, local to the Thanet towns. The opportunity provided by the inaugural run to indulge in some junketings was not missed, six Beauty Queens - Broadstairs, Herne Bay, Kent, Margate, Ramsgate and Whitstable, were in attendance and on arrival at Ramsgate and a reception, speeches, lunch and a coach tour enlivened proceedings.

One facility offered by the service was a seat reservation. In 1948 on Saturdays and Sundays it was the only train on the route where this could be done and even on weekdays there was but one other service on which seats could be reserved. This probably made the train popular and assisted in getting the number of passengers using it in the first three months up to 40,000. Over the period this gave an average of 222 passengers out of a possible 269. The advantage lessened in 1949 when seat reservations were reintroduced on most trains. A small alteration made at this time was for five minutes to be knocked off the 7.10pm arrival at Victoria.

From 1950 a high-season (1st July to 2nd September that year) additional Saturday service was put on each way with departure from Victoria at the early hour, (for an all-Pullman train) of 7.55am, with arrival at Ramsgate at 10.13am, returning from Ramsgate at 11.15am and getting into Victoria at 1.28pm. Stops were made en route at the same points as the other services.

The last run of the THANET BELLE was made on Sunday 24th September 1950, although at the time this was

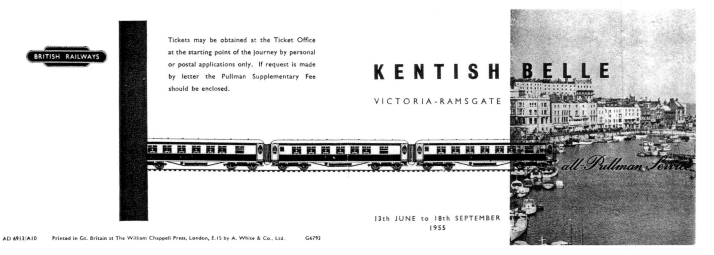

THE KENTISH BELLE

The discerning traveller goes by the BELLES. These are the aristocrats among trains and offer travel-de-luxe for those who like quality. For so little extra cost the passenger gets so much extra comfort. A reserved Pullman seat, refreshments en route (if required), and courteous attention all the way.

So the next time you are going to the Kent Coast remember the KENTISH BELLE. She is the youngest of the four sister trains of the Southern Region, and commenced her career (as the "Thanet Belle") in 1948. But she is very popular, so early booking is essential.

When you travel by the BELLE your journey immediately becomes an enjoyable part of your holiday instead of a mere prelude to it. And all holidays deserve a good beginning and a perfect ending. These you can ensure if you let the BELLE take you there and bring you back.

And while in Kent, why not explore a little. This can be done most economically with one of the 7-day Holiday Runabout Tickets. Two varieties are available (Areas Nos. 1 and 2) at a charge of 12/6 each and leaflets giving details and a map are obtainable at Southern Region stations.

For details of the "Devon Belle," "Brighton Belle" and "Bournemouth Belle," see separate folders.

COMMENCING JUNE 18th UNTIL SEPTEMBER 28th 1951
DOWN

	Mons. to Fris.	Saturdays only.		Suns. only
VICTORIA	11.30 a.m.	7.55 a.m.	3. 6 p.m.	11.30 a.m.
FAVERSHAM	12.43 p.m.	—	—	—
CANTERBURY EAST	1. 6 p.m.	—	—	—
WHITSTABLE & TANKERTON	12.56 p.m.	9.22 a.m.	4.29 p.m.	12.52 p.m.
HERNE BAY	1. 5 p.m.	9.32 a.m.	4.38 p.m.	1. 1 p.m.
MARGATE	1.22 p.m.	9.53 a.m.	4.56 p.m.	1.17 p.m.
BROADSTAIRS	1.33 p.m.	10. 5 a.m.	5. 7 p.m.	1.28 p.m.
RAMSGATE	1.40 p.m.	10.13 a.m.	5.15 p.m.	1.35 p.m.

UP

	Mons. to Fris.	Saturdays only.		Suns. only
RAMSGATE	4.55 p.m.	11.15 a.m.	6.15 p.m.	6.15 p.m.
BROADSTAIRS	5. 1 p.m.	11.22 a.m.	6.21 p.m.	6.21 p.m.
MARGATE	5.10 p.m.	11.32 a.m.	6.30 p.m.	6.30 p.m.
HERNE BAY	5.27 p.m.	11.52 a.m.	6.48 p.m.	6.48 p.m.
WHITSTABLE & TANKERTON	5.36 p.m.	12. 3 p.m.	6.57 p.m.	6.57 p.m.
CANTERBURY EAST	5.30 p.m.	—	—	—
FAVERSHAM	5.53 p.m.	—	—	—
VICTORIA	7. 5 p.m.	1.29 p.m.	8.20 p.m.	8.20 p.m.

(Down and Up tables note: June 30th to Sept. 1st only)

Pullman reservations may be made by personal or postal application at entraining station. If request is made by letter the Pullman Supplementary Fee should be enclosed.

PULLMAN CAR SUPPLEMENTARY FEES

1st Class	3rd Class
s. d.	s. d.
3/6	2/–

AD.6290
BR.35109/5

Printed in Great Britain by McCorquodale, Ldn. S.E.—1172

not widely known, if at all. In the 1951 summer timetable, as part of the Festival of Britain activities, the train was altered to serve Canterbury on Mondays to Fridays in high season. As Canterbury was not part of Thanet a new name had to be found and this was, not unexpectedly, that which had been discarded earlier - KENTISH BELLE. The new timetable had the 11.30am from London calling at Faversham at 12.43pm where it detached three cars, usually two brake thirds (nos 16 and 95) and the first class MAID OF KENT, with a capacity for about 60 passengers. Canterbury East was reached at 1.6pm and the return was made at 5.30pm. The main portion of the train still served Ramsgate and the principal intermediate stations, taking about five minutes longer to reach its destination and having to return ten minutes earlier. At Faversham the Canterbury portion was attached to the rear of the main portion and the combined train left for London at 5.53pm. The result, so far as the Canterbury portion was concerned, could hardly be classified as a success for there were few patrons, and sometimes none at all. Added to which, the stock was worked to and from Faversham empty rather than stand at Canterbury during the afternoon. No locomotive headboard was carried for this portion which had a total of 50 round trips between 2nd July and 7th September. For the August cricket week at Canterbury it was even strengthened with the addition of an extra car, which seemed a huge operating indulgence!

With the Festival past, the 1952 schedules went back to those little removed from 1950, without further amendment to the train's title. Departures from London were at 7.55am on high season Saturdays, 11.35am Mondays to Fridays and Sundays and 3.6pm on Saturdays with corresponding arrivals at Ramsgate and 10.13am, 1.38pm and 5.15pm. Return timings

The Thanet Belle

For Whitstable, Herne Bay Margate, Broadstairs and Ramsgate.

Possibly the rarest picture to have appeared in print for many years, showing the 15.06 Victoria - Ramsgate 'Kentish Belle' on Saturday 30 August 1958 when the power position in London was so acute that nothing larger than an L class 4-4-0 could be found for the service which is seen here near Rainham. *Photograph S.C.Nash.*

78

were 11.15am (high season Saturdays), 5.5pm (Mondays to Friday) and 6.15pm (Saturdays and Sundays), arrivals at Victoria being 1.29pm, 7.5pm and 8.20pm respectively. These carried on until 1957 when small adjustments were made for that year and, it transpired, for 1958, to allow for delays caused by electrification works.

In planning for electrification it had been proposed, in 1956, to discontinue the train. The stock was about 35 years old, of mainly timber construction and required more and more attention. Because the service never produced an overall yearly profit there was little incentive to provide new stock. It would have been possible to continue with electric or diesel-electric haulage but electrification offered a good opportunity to introduce regular interval service, free of the complications of faded luxury running in the summer only. The die was cast on 13th February 1957 when the decision was made to let the train cease at electrification. The final run of the KENTISH BELLE was made with the 6.15pm Ramsgate - Victoria service on 14th September 1958

How the Kentish Belle - referred to the staff on the line as simply 'the Pullman' - looked in its final days. Rebuilt light pacific 34026 YES TOR opens up and accelerates the train away from the extensive Chislehurst Junction relaying slack during the summer of 1958. *Photograph D.W. Winkworth.*

In spite of being perhaps the most prestigious of the Kent coast departures from Victoria, the 15.06 (Saturdays) departed at a time when reserves of locomotives could run low, a situation which resulted in the train occasionally running behind some rather unlikely engines- as was the case on 23 August 1958 when only an N class 2-6-0, No. 31824, was available. This, however, was not the nadir since a week later the train found itself in the hands of an L class 4-4-0. *Photograph R.C. Riley.*

and, if justification was required of the Pullman company and BR for their action, the £2796 loss sustained on the Kentish service that year could be cited. While it can be understood that the weekday timing of the down train was made with a view to obtaining lunch revenue, the short time this gave at the coast was a drawback, nor would it have helped what little business traffic there might have been.

At first ten Pullmans were rostered daily but later this was reduced to eight, other than at the weekends. Motive power was usually a light 4-6-2, usually a Stewarts Lane duty out

and back, although in later years Ramsgate would provide one of the class for some trips. At weekends, when traffic was heavy Schools 4-4-0s would appear and at times of extreme pressure even 2-6-0s of various classes - N or U1 perhaps - or an L 4-4-0 might turn up. Standard class 4-6-0s were seen at times on the eight coach formation mid-week but with the influx of modified light 4-6-2s it became less usual to find any other type working the train, except at weekends. One or more of the Saturday trains eventually were booked for King Arthur 4-6-0s from Ashford shed, to add to

the variety. The 1951 Canterbury portion attracted a lot of lesser classes as it was a Dover duty (No.440) filling-in between bringing other trains to Faversham; 4-4-0s of classes D, D1 and L1 as well as LMR type 2-6-4 tanks could, and did, turn up over this short period.

Pullman trains through Kent, with the possible exception of the GOLDEN ARROW, have never been great money spinners either to the railway or the Pullman company and the THANET cum KENTISH BELLE proved to be no exception.

FOURUM

THE ULSTER CONNECTION ....

Although the major links between Euston and Ireland were via Holyhead (for Eire) and Stranraer (for Ulster), a number of alternatives ran for many years, two of which were the Ulster Express and the Shamrock which ran to Heysham and Liverpool respectively. The Ulster express was a train of long standing and had its origins in the Midland Railway when, in 1904, it inaugurated a St Pancras - Belfast service, leaving London at 18.00 to reach Heysham at 23.52 where the journey was completed by sea. Not only was this a rather circuitous route - 268 miles via Trent and Leeds - but it competed directly with the interests of the L.N.W.R. who operated to Northern Ireland via Liverpool, Stranraer and Fleetwood. The proliferation of services was an early candidate for rationalisation after the merger of the two companies in 1923 - the Heysham service transferring to Euston (although through coaches from St Pancras continued for many years afterwards) at the expense of the Fleetwood service which was allowed to decline. The Ulster Express was one of the earliest L.M.S. named expresses, the train receiving the name in 1927. The Shamrock was a service whose origins were postwar and dated from the tightening up of timings in 1954 when the previous 16.30 service from Euston to Liverpool was retarded by no less than 25 minutes from London but

without any change in the 20.22 arrival in Liverpool. To commemorate the acceleration and because its arrival in Lime Street happened to coincide with the departures of the Night Boats to both Dublin and Belfast, the name 'The Shamrock' was bestowed. In the first of the accompanying illustrations, it appears that on one occasion at least, 7th April 1958, the Ulster Express did not enjoy the best of journeys since in spite of arriving in Euston behind Coronation Pacific 46257 CITY OF SALFORD and not the booked 7P 4-6-0, it appears to have been at least an hour late, the booked arrival time being 11.35. In the second picture an engine of the booked type, rebuilt Patriot 4-6-0 45545 PLANET takes advantage of the falling gradient from

Tring as it rushes the express out of Watford tunnel and on to London. When things went to plan the Shamrock enjoyed a more illustrious form of motive power than the Ulster Express and was booked to be worked by an Edge Hill (8A) Princess Royal Pacific: a type not over-common on services south of Crewe. In the third view the booked engine, Princess Royal 46204 PRINCESS LOUISE eases the train over the down slow lines at Camden preparatory to applying the brakes for the sharp descent into Euston. In the final scene, there are suggestions of motive power problems at Edge Hill as Royal Scot 4-6-0 46110 GRENADIER GUARDSMAN has been substituted for the diagrammed Princess Royal Pacific.

Photograph D.C.Ovenden.

NEWTON ABBOT AND THE MORETONHAMPSTEAD BRANCH

I.C. COLEFORD

Newton Abbot was once the home of the South Devon Railway, which opened the Exeter - Newton Abbot section of its line on 30 December 1846. The line was extended southwards to Totnes on 20 July 1847 and reached Plymouth on 5 May 1848. Newton Abbot became a junction on 18 December 1848 when a branch to Torre (Torquay) came, eventually extending to Kingswear, and the railway map of Newton Abbot was virtually completed on 4 July 1866 when the branch to Moretonhampstead was opened.

The South Devon Railway was a broad gauge concern, and is partly remembered for its unsuccessful attempt at atmospheric traction instead of conventional locomotive haulage. The atmospheric system, which had been developed by the Samuda Brothers in 1840, involved the laying of a cast iron pipe between the rails, and the provision of stationary pumping houses at regular intervals along the line to pump air through the pipe. Each 'locomotive' was fitted with a piston which was propelled through the pipe by the action of air pressure pushing against a vacuum. The SDR opted for this on the advice of its engineer, Isambard Kingdom Brunel, who considered that it would be faster, quieter, create no pollution from coke dust, and result in a saving of £8,000 pa on locomotive expenses.

Brunel's enthusiasm for the novel form of traction was encapsulated in his report that:

'....I have no hesitation in taking upon myself the full and entire responsibility of recommending the adoption of the Atmospheric System on the South Devon Railway, and of recommending as a consequence that the line and works should be constructed for a single line only'.

Brunel's idea was for the SDR to use 15in-diameter pipes for the northern section of the Exeter - Plymouth line, and 221/2 in diameter pipes on the more heavily graded sections in the south. The laying of only a single line, incidentally, proved extremely troublesome after the abandonment of the atmospheric system, and the doubling of the entire Exeter - Plymouth line was not completed until 1905. Much has been written elsewhere about the failings of the atmospheric system but, in a nutshell, its major problem was the use of leather in the valves of, firstly, the pipes and, secondly, the pistons of the 'locomotives'. It was soon found that the vacuum created by the pumping of air dried out the natural oil of the leather, thereby making the seals very vulnerable to intruding rain or frost. The remedy of applying additional grease was, however, found to provide little more than a gastronomic treat for rats. A knock-on effect was that, when the leather started breaking up, more pumping was required to obtain the same vacuum, and the pumping houses were therefore required to work beyond their capabilities. Consequently, failures in the pumping houses became increasingly frequent.

The atmospheric trains only ever worked on the Exeter - Newton Abbot

This creased and battered view of the southern approaches to Newton Abbot station would probably have been taken in the early 1920s since the station is clearly in its pre-1920s rebuilding form whilst the locomotive immediately to the right of the station appears to be a ROD 2-8-0; a type not introduced on the GWR until May 1919. The engine shed and works are just about discernible in the distance on the right-hand side of the frame. The coaching stock in the foreground - one six wheel brake, two four wheelers and what looks like a four wheeled clerestory - might prompt a comment or two from rolling stock experts. *Photograph John Smith.*

section, and were formally abandoned on 10 September 1848. The 'atmospheric caper', as it had become known, had, by then, cost the SDR in excess of £400,000. It was one of the comparatively few blots on Brunel's career.

At Newton Abbot the original station had its Up and Down platforms on the same side of the line, a similar unorthodox arrangement being used by the neighbouring Bristol & Exeter Railway at Exeter and Taunton. Newton Abbot station was rebuilt in a slightly less idiosynchratic style in 1861, albeit with three roads but five platform faces. This layout meant that there were platform faces on both sides of two of the roads, thereby enabling passengers to alight from either side of carriages. The idea behind this was to make things easier for passengers wishing to change trains, a saunter across the width of a platform being more agreeable than a hike across a footbridge, and similar arrangements were still to be found elsewhere in the 1960s. At Newton Abbot station, this was particularly useful for passengers changing to or from trains on the Torquay 'branch'. The South Devon Railway was absorbed by the GWR on 1 February 1876, but its former lines remained a bastion of the broad gauge until the long weekend of 20-23 May 1892. By the early 1900s the traffic using Newton Abbot station had increased sig-

Newton Abbot station from the south, once again. This picture appears to show the layout in its final form before the 1920s reconstruction - the building with the chimneys to the right is the carriage and wagon workshop. *Photograph Lens of Sutton.*

nificantly, partly due to the Torbay area's growth in popularity as a holiday resort. However, the layout at the station became a positive hindrance to smooth operations—particularly during the peak summer season—as the availability of only one Down road and the lack of a through road created a major bottleneck. Matters were not fully addressed until the early 1920s, the 'GWR Magazine' of May 1923 explaining that:

This well-known picture, taken from the northern end of Newton Abbot station on 12 June 1920, shows Saint class 4-6-0 2978 KIRKLAND, a locomotive which had started life in 1905 as No.178. It has sometimes been stated that the engine was named after a GWR director, but the owner of the name would have looked a little out of place in the corridors of power at Paddington as Kirkland was, in fact, a racehorse owned by GWR director Frank Bibby. Those with a knowledge of the turf will, of course, be familiar with the fact that the creature won the Grand National in 1907. 2978 had been in Swindon Works since late 1919 and when released on 16 May 1920, was allocated to Newton Abbot shed where it spent the rest of the year (and more). In May 1935 it was renamed CHARLES J HAMBRO. *Photograph Lens of Sutton.*

These two early 1920s views of the original station (from the southern end) show that modernisation was clearly overdue. The assortment of enamel signs is fascinating; many of the products advertised still being available today. It could be asked whether Iron Jelloids were claimed to assist in the climbing of stairs. The cobbled surface of the down platform is clearly evident as is the stone construction of the island platform and it is probable that the faces of the platforms saw some alterations with the demise of the broad gauge. The overwhelming impression given by these pictures is that every movement in the station must have echoed tremedously.

'Some idea of the growth of the town will be realised when it is stated that in the past fifty years the population has doubled... The industry of Newton Abbot, which is rapidly extending, is at present chiefly represented by six china clay works, three granite quarries, and four potteries. Newton Abbot is also one of the principal cider distributing centres in Devon, and is likely to be the centre for the distribution of electricity to the surrounding districts.

'Newton Abbot has been described

as the "Key to the West Country", but when it is stated that the railway station is one of the few survivals of the works of the great engineer Brunel, it will be realised that the key is of somewhat antiquated pattern. Alterations have been carried out from time to time, but parts of the old structure still remain, and over the three main exits wrought-iron scrolls inscribed "South Devon Railway" are to be seen today.

'Schemes for a new station have been under consideration for a long

while. But for the war the much-needed improvements would undoubtedly have been carried out some years ago. The work is now to be put in hand, however, and the inevitable delay is not without its advantages, as it has enabled the Company to introduce the latest improvements, both in the station architecture and the planning of station accommodation'.

The article then proceeded to explain how the GWR planned to give the town better rail facilities:

The approved proposals will result in the construction of a station that will cost close upon £250,000. The final cost was, in fact, £247,100.

'At present there are only two Up and one Down platform lines available for through trains, whilst the longest platform is only 669 feet long. A census taken last summer revealed that apart from excursions, as many as 147 passenger and 60 goods trains passed through or stopped at the station in one day.

The plans for the new station comprise:
Additional platform accommodation;
Improved booking and parcels offices, and cloak room;
Commodious footbridge for passengers, with separate bridge and electric lifts for luggage and passengers;
Improvement of permanent-way and provision of additional sidings;
Independent platform for Moretonhampstead branch trains.
New 65-feet turntable in the locomotive depot, for turning the largest engines in use on the system.
Electricity for lighting to be installed throughout the station.
The main station buildings, including a commodious dining room and a large booking hall will be situated on the Up side of the line.
'At the new Up "island" platform what is known as a "scissors" crossing will be provided. This will enable two trains to be dealt with at the same time.

Among the contracts let, the GWR Traffic Committee's minutes for 17 December 1925 noted the following: 'With J. Tildesley Ltd for covered footbridge and platform coverings at Newton Abbot: £17,457. 19s. 4d. With A.N. Coles & Son Ltd for new booking hall and buildings at Newton Abbot, on approximate quantities to be furnished by the Company - not exceeding £36,465'

While the rebuilding work was in hand, Aller Junction (to the south of Newton Abbot at the point where the Torbay line diverged) was completely remodelled to provide Up and Down main and relief lines. Previously, Torbay trains had used separate lines parallel to the Newton Abbot - Plymouth main line - a similar arrangement to that which exists today.

The new station was formally opened by Lord Mildmay of Flete on Monday 11 April 1927, the new arrangement including eight designated platform faces (on two island platforms) and two roads for non-stop workings. From the east, they were:

Table 1								
	STAFF		TICKETS		RECEIPTS			
Year	No.	Paybill	Issues	Season	Passengers	Parcels	Misc	Total
1903	na	6,350	246,451	na	19,716	2,330	1,462	23,508
1913	129	9,069	297,629	na	24,351	2,015	1,299	27,665
1923	172	29,522	343,079	1,626	43,035	1,717	2,119	46,871
1929	184	32,825	265,858	1,865	40,832	4,008	2,571	47,411
1930	187	33,940	247,753	1,788	39,619	4,005	2,347	45,971
1931	186	32,369	238,747	2,353	37,307	3,690	2,058	43,055
1932	181	30,197	229,320	2,712	34,738	3,584	1,854	40,176
1933	175	30,432	221,936	3,135	33,965	3,526	1,969	39,460
1934	174	30,824	208,951	3,110	32,554	3,673	2,028	38,255

NEWTON ABBOT . (PASSENGER TRAFFIC)

Down through road
Down relief - platforms 1 and 2
Down main - platforms 3 and 4
Up relief - platforms 5 and 6
Up main - platforms 7 and 8
Up through road

The opening of the 'new' station was duly reported in the railway press of the day, the following account appearing in the June 1927 issue of the 'Railway Magazine':

'....Interesting reminders of bygone days are the wrought-iron scrolls, inscribed "S.D.R.", (South Devon Railway) which had to be removed from above the old exits. These are being preserved, one over the ticket windows in the main booking hall of the new station, one in the Newton Abbot Museum, and the other among the historic relics at Paddington.

'Work on the new station was commenced in November 1924. An imposing, three-storey, block of buildings has been erected on the main Newton Abbot - Torquay road, facing the town park. The structure is of Portland stone and red Somerset bricks. A conspicuous feature of the pleasing facade is a handsome clock, placed in the centre pediment, the gift of the townspeople of Newton Abbot. (The local interest in the station redevelopment was to be expected as Newton Abbot was very much a 'Railway Town'; as mentioned in the article on the engine shed and works in BRILL 3.7, around 1,000 local men relied on the railway for their employment in the late 1930s, some railwaymen becoming councillors and even mayors).

'The three small platforms which formerly served the station have been replaced by two wide island platforms, each having a length of 1,375ft, of which 570ft is veranda covered. A separate bay platform of 320ft has been provided to meet the increasing traffic over the Moretonhampstead branch. (That was platform nine, with separate access only from the station forecourt - the reference to 'increasing traffic' on the Moretonhampstead branch might seem to be contradicted by the accompanying tables, but prior to 1923 return tickets were counted as two singles, hence the apparently impressive 'tickets issued' figures for 1903 and 1913.) Alterations have also been made in regard to the running lines, so that there are now six running lines (through, main, and relief) with scissors crossings intermediately along the platforms. Four lines, arranged on the parallel system, have been provided as far as Aller Junction.

'Two new manual signal-boxes have been constructed at the east and west ends of the station, in place of the three previously existing, (the old Middle box was the casualty) and it is of interest to note that one of them contains 206 levers, and is, therefore, the second largest manual box on the system.

'Refreshment rooms are available on each platform, also centrally-placed waiting rooms and attractive bookstalls. The station is lighted by electricity, and all the buildings are centrally heated. On the first floor is a dining and tea room, 66ft by 19ft. This room will be available for social functions, and has a separate entrance with staircase, which gives direct access to and from the street. There is a new telegraph office, and improved accommodation has been provided for the station master, inspectors, and other staff'.

The work in progress at the southern end of Newton Abbot station is to prepare the way for the new up platform, which was to extend virtually to the West signal box (seen on the right of the frame). The carriage & wagon works, with its distinctive rake of chimneys, is clearly visible in the middle-distance.

Table 2															
	MORETONHAMPSTEAD			LUSTLEIGH			BOVEY			HEATHFIELD			TEIGNGRACE		
Year	Total	Wages	Receipts	Total	Wages	Receipts	Total	Wages	Receipts	Total	Wages	Receipts	Total	Wages	Receipts
1903	7	395	9,139	2	99	1,808	5	235	8,056	6	281	7,189	1	78	268
1913	8	502	10,985	2	126	2,111	5	330	9,956	6	342	5,877	1	72	219
1923	9	1,472	14,450	2	350	3,036	6	868	11,310	7	954	18,475	1	154	223
1929	9	1.359	12,370	2	292	2,291	6	968	10,342	9	1,184	18,052	na	na	136
1930	9	1,327	11,268	2	311	2,123	6	988	9,982	9	885	16,515	na	na	103
1931	9	1,306	10,213	2	216	1,872	6	970	9,866	9	1,056	15,921	na	na	81
1932	9	1,291	8,605	2	230	1,731	6	954	8,837	10	1,037	15,606	na	na	100
1933	9	1,423	8,743	2	246	1,899	6	1,038	8,691	10	1,111	17,996	na	na	86
1934	9	1,427	8,708	2	246	1,760	6	1,043	9,585	10	1,130	20,452	na	na	75

MORETONHAMPSTEAD BRANCH : INCOME AND EXPENDITURE

Figues for Brimley and Hawkmoor halts are included with Bovey. All wages and receipts in £'s.

This 'rebuilding' picture shows that the old island platform has been virtually demolished. The dismantling of the overall roof has commenced and, perhaps prematurely, the new sign for the Moretonhampstead branch platform (No.9) has already been delivered. The point at which the 'Platform 9' sign is resting was once the site of three short spurs which were conneced to the main line by means of a wagon turntable - the alterations are evidenced by the different construction of the platform at this point.

The reference to the provision of scissors crossings (to the relief roads between the platforms) is interesting. In theory this enabled eight main-line trains to be accommodated at the station simultaneously, but in practice the scissors crossings were used only infrequently as they were considered to be a possible safety hazard. One omission from the above report was a mention that the preserved ex-SDR broad gauge locomotive TINY, a vertical boilered 0-4-0WT built by Sara & Co of Plymouth in 1868, was placed on display on the new Down platform. It remained there until acquired by the Dart Valley Railway in 1980, and has the proud status of being the one and only surviving broad gauge locomotive.

Over the years, Newton Abbot station accommodated a huge cross-section of GWR motive power - and some non-GWR types as well. The express services were entrusted to Swindon's finest - the 'Bulldog' and other types of 4-4-0s of the 1890s/early 1900s gradually giving way to 'Saint' class 4-6-0s which, in turn, were joined by the four-cylinder 'Stars' and, ultimately, the 'Castles' and the 'Kings'.

Among the expresses routed through Newton Abbot were the 'Cornish Riviera', introduced in 1904 with what was the longest scheduled non-stop run in the world, the 'Torbay Express'—formally inaugurated in 1923,

the short-lived 'Torbay Pullman' of 1929/30, the 'Cornishman'—officially introduced for a brief period in 1935 despite dating back to broad gauge days (and resuscitated in 1952, albeit for the Wolverhampton - Penzance service), and also the Bradford - Paignton/Kingswear 'Devonian'. Later additions were the 'Royal Duchy' and the 'Mayflower', while in diesel days the 'Armada' and the 'Night Riviera' materialised.

From the early 1900s local passenger services were worked mainly by 2-6-2Ts, the '3150s' eventually giving way to the '5101s' whereas the '4400' and '4500s' retained a distinct presence in and around Newton Abbot vir-

Table 3							MORETONHAMPSTEAD. TRAFFIC STATISTICS										
	Tickets		Receipts				FORWARDED (tons)			RECEIVED (tons)			Coal	TOTALS			L'stock
Year	Issues	Season	Pass	Parcels	Misc	Total	Coal	Mins	General	Coal	Mins	General	(free))	Tons	Receipts	Carted	(Vans)
1903	30,292	na	3,232	1,071	582	4,885	9	488	2,185	1,399	2,158	5,109	2,438	13,786	4,254	1,551	202
1913	47,666	na	4,472	1,048	436	5,956	-	50	2,165	557	2,165	5,572	4,403	14,653	5,029	1,776	324
1923	28,323	163	4,428	1,117	571	6,116	26	95	3,709	626	3,709	4,328	4,066	14,876	8,334	1,379	307
1929	18,687	118	2,682	1,096	786	4,564	19	71	2,583	542	2,583	3,739	4,711	13,736	7,806	1,212	263
1930	15,756	158	2,360	1,082	793	4,235	-	32	3,404	769	3,404	3,212	4,600	13,423	7,033	1,049	177
1931	14,214	150	2,151	977	611	3,739	-	58	1,888	621	1,888	3,171	4,963	12,369	6,474	1,028	104
1932	13,517	179	1,950	822	327	3,099	-	70	1,417	534	1,417	2,690	4,831	10,426	5,506	983	85
1933	12,099	212	1,629	732	405	2,766	6	92	1,398	595	1,398	2,779	4,707	10,559	5,977	1,684	114
1934	11,990	170	1,556	831	580	2,967	-	49	985	494	985	3,006	4,578	9,835	5,741	1,841	139

tually throughout their entire lives. Secondary and freight workings enjoyed the attentions of almost everything ranging from 0-6-0ST/PTs and 2-6-0s to 2-8-0s and the later two-cylinder mixed traffic 4-6-0s. The banking engines for Dainton and Rattery also dwelt at Newton Abbot, and during the war '7200' 2-8-2Ts were introduced on those duties. That said, the official allocation lists show that Newton Abbot shed had only one 2-8-2T - 7222 - on its books, but 7200, 7220 and 7250 were listed as redidents on 1 January 1948.

It would be impossible to give comprehensive details of every type of locomotive ever seen at Newton Abbot, though as a hopefully acceptable and nostalgic alternative, I have perused the relevant pages of 'Trains Illustrated' (a.k.a. 'Motive Power Miscellany') for a random selection of less-than-common sightings at Newton Abbot during the 1950s. Among the reports from the trusty band of correspondents in 1952 were:

'On 4/3/52 Metro-Vick gas turbine No.18100 worked a 12-coach 360-ton train from Swindon to Plymouth and back, and on 6/3/52, over the same route, a 17-coach, 520-ton train, which was successfully restarted on Hemerdon bank....On 15/4/52 the advance part of the "Cornish Riviera" suffered a failure at Newton Abbot, where "Castle" No.4098 replaced "County" No.1000... On 23/5/52 2-8-2T No.7250 worked the 8.5am Kingswear-Exeter passenger on from Torquay after "Castle" No.5011 had been taken off owing to vacuum brake trouble (No 7250 was due to enter Newton Abbot works the next day for a 'light casual'). Notable sights at Newton Abbot on 19/7/52 included Shrewsbury "Star" No.4044 heading the 2.55pm Paignton-Wolverhampton, and Stafford Road "Star" No.4049 on the 10.18am Wolverhampton - Paignton..."King" No6018 hauled the LMS Royal Train from Paddington at 10.30am when HM The Queen visited the Royal Show at Newton Abbot on 2/7/52'.

One extract from the May 1954 issue referred to 'Dukedog' 4-4-0 No 9023, tried as a pilot between Newton Abbot and Plymouth, the outcome of its exertions being that it was promptly sent home. Jumping ahead to 1955, the same periodical reported:

'One of Exmouth Junction's "3MT" 2-6-2Ts, No.82022, has been working through Newton Abbot en-route between

Using the angle of lighting as a guide, it is safe to say that this picture of Newton Abbot station was taken at 5.50pm on a date shortly after the reconstruction of the 1920s had been completed. *Photograph Lens of Sutton.*

Exeter and Plymouth on 15 and 16/12/ 54... An unusual double-heading was observed on 16/12/54 when "King" No.6000 assisted "County" No.1000 from Newton Abbot to Plymouth with the down "Cornish Riviera Express" ...new "3MT" 2-6-2Ts Nos.82033/34 have gone to Newton Abbot, and have been noted on Torquay branch passenger work and also on banking duty over the South Devon inclines (May issue) ...Five of the new "3MT" 2-6-2Ts, Nos.82004/ 09/31/33/34, are now at Newton Abbot for banking and branch duties; engines displaced by the new arrivals are light 2-6-2Ts Nos.5543/52/57 (June issue) ...The LM Pacific on loan to the WR for tests, No.46327, was seen at Newton Abbot on 10/5/55 when it was making its first trip to Plymouth with the 9.30am from Paddington....The new "3MT" 2-6-2Ts are employed on many Kingswear line stopping trains from Newton Abbot and Exeter (September issue) ...On 13/7/55 2-6-0 No.6372 was seen at Newton Abbot with the Down "Riviera", having replaced "King" No.6008 at Exeter'.

Later on in the 1950s the observation team noted:

'Newton Abbot (shed) again has a share in the working of the "Torbay

Express", providing the engine for the Down train on Tuesdays, Thursdays and Saturdays (December 1956 issue).. Withdrawn ex-Taff Vale 0-6-2T No.361 arrived at Newton Abbot, apparently for its boiler to be transferred to 2-6-2T No.4547 (June 1957 issue)... Employed on Dainton bank after repair at Newton Abbot were 0-6-2Ts Nos.5696 (86D) and 6600 (86C) (July 1957 issue)... On 21/11/58 "9F" No.92006 (86A) headed the 3.5pm coal empties from Hackney (Newton Abbot) to Bassaleg... On 20/12/58 No.92238 was noted heading the 7.0pm Newton Abbot - Acton fitted freight.. For the summer service (of 1959) "Manor" 4-6-0s have been drafted to Newton Abbot and Laira (the first 'Manors' to be allocated to Newton Abbot, incidentally, were 7813 on 13 May 1948, 7814 on 7 June 1948, and 7805 on 21 September 1950))... On 26/6/59 SR Pacific No.34033 worked to Totnes, piloted from Newton Abbot by a 2-6-2T, with an excursion from Torrington (SR 'West Countries' had regularly worked through Newton Abbot from the late 1940s to the late 1950s on exchange workings—normally two trains each way on weekdays; before the Pacifics, 'N' class 2-6-0s had undertaken those

Table 4							LUSTLEIGH. TRAFFIC STATISTICS										
	Tickets		Receipts				FORWARDED (tons)			RECEIVED (tons)			Coal	TOTALS			L'stock
Year	Issues	Season	Pass	Parcels	Misc	Total	Coal	Mins	General	Coal	Mins	General	(free))	Tons	Receipts	Carted	(Vans)
1903	16,898	na	961	257	97	1,315	-	-	675	456	799	402	183	2,515	583	225	-
1913	16,986	na	1,095	294	79	1,468	-	-	494	13	592	506	766	2,371	643	317	-
1923	19,710	64	1,764	184	73	2,021	8	13	785	114	209	400	867	2,396	1,015	224	-
1929	16,461	80	1,332	156	25	1,513	13	-	423	258	27	337	904	1,962	778	87	-
1930	15,137	86	1,223	140	30	1,393	-	7	524	75	112	269	1,201	2,188	730	68	-
1931	14,587	102	1,204	91	12	1,307	-	32	230	48	121	237	1,139	1,807	565	69	-
1932	13,947	103	1,073	81	20	1,174	-	-	217	79	72	284	1,114	1,766	557	103	-
1933	13,458	126	1,077	78	26	1,181	-	-	278	68	277	307	1,081	2,011	718	199	-
1934	12,662	199	1,033	79	92	1,204	-	-	195	74	86	265	1,050	1,670	556	168	-

A marvellous photograph showing a gleaming 2-6-2T 5557 which is known to have been a Newton Abbot engine for at least part of the late 1940s and this helps to confirm the approximate date of the picture. The train, presumably an up local, waits at Platform 7, the engine having just backed on as the fireman is in the process in reversing the headlamps. The Moretonhampstead branch platform is out of view to the right of the picture.

duties) ....On 4/7/59 No.92205 passed through Newton Abbot with the 7.35am Plymouth - Paddington passenger train....On 27/7/59 the "Torbay Express" was absorbed into the Laira diesel rosters.. The WR 2-10-0s graduated to named train working in August, for an observer at Newton Abbot on 8/8/59 reported No.92206 (83D) on the Up "Mayflower"... A regular item of Saturday working this summer (1959) has been a combination of two "Manors" on the 6am Penzance - Crewe between Plymouth and Newton Abbot.. On 15/8/59 "King" No.6018 was coupled ahead of diesel No.D802 at Newton Abbot on the 10.35am Paddington - Penzance - the impression gained elsewhere is that

this was a practice to be avoided to prevent fouling the diesel's air intakes...."King" No.6011 of Stafford Road now works the 9.05am Liverpool - Plymouth between Shrewsbury and Newton Abbot on Mondays, Wednesdays and Fridays' (December 1959).

The later reports quoted above contained the first real evidence of long-term changes. Inevitably, the Western Region's fleet of diesels increased and the use of steam traction diminished accordingly - by the end of 1963 steam had been virtually eliminated west of Exeter. The main line trains through Newton Abbot continued to do reasonable business although, of course, the huge increase in car ownership in the

1950s and 1960s made a significant dent in the receipts.

As for Newton Abbot station itself, track simplification work was undertaken between 1968 and 1976. It involved the removal of intermediate crossovers and the rationalisation of platform numbering, Nos 1 and 2 becoming Platform 1, Nos 3 and 4 becoming Platform 2, Nos 5 and 6 becoming Platform 3, and Nos 7 and 8 becoming platform 4. By then, the branch platform (No 9) had long been disused, although it is still served by a siding today. Further remodelling was undertaken in 1987, platforms 1, 2 and 3 being made 'reversible' and designated respectively: Down/Up relief,

Table 5							BOVEY	TRAFFIC	STATISTICS								
	Tickets		Receipts				FORWARDED (tons)			RECEIVED (tons)			Coal		TOTALS			L'stock
Year	Issues	Season	Pass	Parcels	Misc	Total	Coal	Mins	General	Coal	Mins	General	(free))	Tons	Receipts	Carted	(Vans)
1903	38,297	na	2,172	501	223	2,896	41	68	1,636	6,493	3,797	3,339	499	15,873	5,160	1,435	3
1913	34,646	na	2,581	383	75	3,039	38	1,444	2,200	3,435	5,213	4,518	4,290	21,138	6,917	1,837	5
1923	28,756	113	3,644	393	96	4,133	7	46	1,563	1,483	1,334	3,938	4,889	13,215	7,177	1,625	4
1929	16,397	181	1,996	920	323	3,239	25	91	1,308	941	1,904	3,295	6,889	14,459	7,103	1,621	7
1930	15,023	281	1,883	901	342	3,126	18	52	1,303	1,042	2,132	3,033	6,121	13,701	6,856	1,507	1
1931	14,949	183	1,625	857	236	2,718	-	41	1,337	929	1,452	3,630	5,300	12,689	7,148	1,427	3
1932	15,166	207	1,615	835	223	2,673	-	35	878	989	1,334	3,122	5,586	11,944	6,164	1,656	2
1933	14,546	180	1,691	853	161	2,705	-	60	968	668	1,315	2,787	5,765	11,563	5,986	2,031	6
1934	13,961	165	1,690	789	150	2,629	16	53	962	575	1,546	3,133	6,024	12,309	6,956	2,724	13

Receipts from Brimley and Hawkmoor Halts are included from 1928 and 1931 respectively

Table 6							HEATHFIELD. TRAFFIC STATISTICS										
	Tickets		Receipts				FORWARDED (tons)			RECEIVED (tons)			Coal	TOTALS			L'stock
Year	Issues	Season	Pass	Parcels	Misc	Total	Coal	Mins	General	Coal	Mins	General	(free))	Tons	Receipts	Carted	(Vans)
1903	12,344	na	639	64	20	723	-	11,239	3,582	261	13,171	482	6,703	35,438	6,466	227	-
1913	11,575	na	643	59	25	727	-	3,922	4,573	1,107	10,687	688	5,733	26,620	5,150	973	1
1923	13,346	61	946	98	89	1,133	-	8,500	5,115	3,644	3,364	1,153	3,265	25,041	17,342	3,104	1
1929	22,379	51	896	171	25	1,092	-	3,472	5,723	1,139	5,279	1,156	4,410	21,179	16,960	3,411	-
1930	21,676	43	751	178	51	980	-	3,210	5,374	457	989	1,149	4,915	16,094	15,535	3,178	-
1931	21,610	63	759	170	41	970	5	3,410	5,360	650	766	1,112	4,293	15,596	14,951	3,025	-
1932	20,072	65	772	145	6	923	-	2,948	4,711	950	1,865	1,013	4,197	15,684	14,683	3,127	-
1933	20,719	84	858	151	19	1,028	-	3,442	4,931	2,353	670	1,250	3,071	15,717	16,968	3,473	-
1934	21,984	80	819	158	8	985	-	2,283	6,360	2,565	603	1,422	4,557	18,790	19,467	3,576	-

44xx class 2-6-2T 4405 arrives at Newton Abbot with a local goods from the south, possibly from Ashburton, in June 1953. The engine spent several years at Newton Abbot, being withdrawn from there in September 1955. *Photograph J.Davenport.*

The pre-nationalisation ownership of 2-6-2T 4547 needs little advertising despite the faded lettering on the side-tanks. Unfortunately details of the train being worked are missing although the sandwiching of an engine between an auto-coach and an ordinary vehicle on platform 9 might suggest a commonplace shunting movement. *Photograph R.Carpenter.*

Down main, Up main. All were short-ened at the west end. Platform 4 dis-appeared and, with the Up through road also closed, much of the area va-cated was redeveloped as a car park.

During the steam era - especially on summer Saturdays - Newton Abbot was indeed a useful place for filling in blanks in the Combined Volume. Most of the activity was, of course, on through workings to or from the Torbay line, Plymouth or Cornwall, but for those with an interest in more sedate goings-on, Platform 9 of Newton Ab-bot station was the arrival and depar-ture point of trains on the Moretonhampstead branch and also the few that had worked through from the Teign Valley line. This admittedly lame attempt at continuity is, in fact, a way of saying that we're now going to have a look at the Moretonhampstead branch.

Newton Abbot - Moretonhampstead

In parts of the West Country, the broad gauge railway companies - the Great Western, Bristol & Exeter, and South Devon Railways - considered the standard gauge London & South West-ern Railway to be the proverbial thorn in the side. The L&SWR was rather keen on the prospect of extending westwards from Exeter, and made highly dubious use of so-called 'inde-pendent' railway companies to further its aims. One thinly-veiled L&SWR subsidiary was the Devon Central Rail-way which, in 1861, presented a bill for a line from Exeter to Lydford (or *Lidford* as it was then spelt) via Moretonhampstead, Chagford and Okehampton.

The 'Devon Central' proposal failed to gain Assent, but it set the alarm bells ringing in the broad gauge camp. The outcome was the incorporation on 7 July 1862 of the Moretonhampstead & South Devon Railway—a nominally independent concern chaired by the Earl of Devon, but with the SDR hold-ing a controlling interest. The M&SDR comprised a 12 1/4 mile branch from Newton Abbot to Moretonhampstead, the line being built to the broad gauge as of necessity as it was to be worked by the SDR in return for 50% of gross re-ceipts.

Among the surviving minutes of the M&SDR is the report (of 1863?) that: *'The South Devon Railway would not subscribe any of the Capital, but Mr Woollcombe (Chairman of the SDR and named as a director of the M&SDR) would not object as an Individual to subscribe £500 provided that the Land-owners acted in a liberal spirit in giv-ing their lands on easy terms, and tak-ing their proper share in raising the Capital. Mr Woollcombe thought that if £1,000 a mile was raised locally there might be no difficulty in carrying the matter out.'*

An extract from the minutes of a meeting of 7 February 1866 explained that: *'Mr Margery* (Peter Margery, Brunel's former assistant during the construction of the SDR, who had taken over as the SDR's Chief Engi-

In this undated picture, 2-6-2T 4555 (now preserved) is arriving at Newton Abbot station with a local goods working. The signal box is the West Box and its siting can be compared with that in one of the 'rebuilding' photographs. *Photograph Terry Nicholls.*

Potteries. Mr Margery submitted plans and estimates which he had had prepared after careful examination and explained the grounds upon which he had arrived at the conclusion that it would be advisable to construct two sidings instead of one for the purposes of both parties as had been suggested by the Duke of Somerset's Agent.

'Mr Divett then urged that a portion of the cost of constructing the Pottery siding should be borne by the Company'.

The branch opened on 4 July 1866, the initial estimate of construction costs - £88,500 - having proved to be a tiny bit on the optimistic side, as the final bill worked out at £140,000. The 'independent' life of the Moretonhampstead & South Devon Railway came to an end in 1872 when it was formally absorbed by the SDR. The SDR was itself absorbed by the GWR in 1876, and the branch was converted to the standard gauge in May 1892.

Although relations between the M&SDR and the SDR had, on the whole, been cordial, an M&SDR minute of 31 August 1867 betrayed a bone of contention: 'Read letters... from Mr Ser-

neer after Brunel's death in 1859) reported that in consequence of the Contractors declining to supply rails and timber for sidings at the Stations, and the same not being included in their original Contract, it would be necessary for the Company to provide the materials themselves, and that he estimated the cost of the same at £1,200'.

On 2 June 1866, the matter of water came under discussion: 'The Secretary reported that in order to obtain a supply of water for the Moreton station without the permanent cost of pumping, it had been found necessary to negotiate with Mr John Harvey of Budleigh (the lessee of a farm under the Earl of Devon) and that Mr Drew had offered to allow the Company to lay down pipes through his Lordship's property on payment of a yearly rent of £5, the same to be paid to Mr Harvey during the continuance of his lease, and that the South Devon Co were willing to contribute £100 towards the cost of the pipes provided the proposed arrangement should be approved by this Board'.

Sidings were discussed on 13 August 1866: 'The Secretary having reported that the Haytor Granite Quarry was now being worked (an unexpected revival?) and that the Duke of Somerset had called upon the Company to construct

2-6-2T 4150 passes Newton Abbot East with a train of loco coal from Hackney Yard on 15 July 1959. *Photograph R.C.Riley.*

the Siding near the Bovey Potteries, in accordance with the agreement, and also that Mr Divett (owner of the potteries and a director of the M&SDR) was desirous of having a siding into the

geant (Secretary and General Manager of the SDR) specifying certain works which the South Devon Company required to be executed as the conditions on which they would undertake the

Table 7							TEIGNGRACE. TRAFFIC STATISTICS									
	Tickets		Receipts				FORWARDED (tons)			RECEIVED (tons)			Coal	TOTALS			L'stock
Year	Issues	Season	Pass	Parcels	Misc	Total	Coal	Mins	General	Coal	Mins	General	(free))	Tons	Receipts	Carted	(Vans)
1903	4,808	na	120	29	20	169	-	-	1	187	174	91	-	453	99	1	-
1913	3,519	na	106	23	-	129	-	-	4	133	305	83	79	604	90	3	-
1923	3,125	-	99	11	5	115	-	-	19	-	273	30	-	322	108	17	-
1929	1,869	8	62	5	14	81	-	-	-	-	430	9	12	441	55	1	-
1930	1,415	1	52	5	15	72	-	-	-	-	331	8	11	350	31	-	-
1931	1,316	4	50	2	12	64	-	-	-	-	17	1	-	18	17	1	-
1932	1,425	-	52	2	21	75	-	-	-	-	25	1	-	26	25	1	-
1933	1,234	-	40	7	24	71	-	-	1	-	-	9	-	10	15	1	-
1934	1,193	-	40	2	12	54	-	-	-	-	130	-	-	130	21	-	-

Another Newton Abbot 2-6-2T, 5150, waits at Platform 4 with a six-coach southbound local on 18 April 1960. The engine was withdrawn only four months later. As is evident the even numbers of the dual-designated platform faces (Nos 2,4,6 and 8) were at the southern end of the station. *Photograph Stephen Gradidge.*

'Matchbox' 9487 was on station pilot duty at Newton Abbot on 13 June 1959. The engine was one of many which had a very brief life, being built in November 1952 and going to the breakers yard in July 1962. The predomination of 2-6-2Ts on shed will be noted. *Photograph Terry Nicholls.*

maintenance of the line. The Secretary reported that the Engineer having advised that the greater part of these works properly devolved on the Contractors, he had written to them requiring them to execute the same, and had received a letter in reply, in which they stated that they distinctly declined to carry out the requisitions'.

It appears that, a few years later, there had been a problem with an unpaid bill (albeit not with the SDR) the subject being discussed on 29 June 1870: 'The Secretary reported that the Electric Telegraph Co had commenced proceedings with the view of recovering their debt of £292. 8s. 7d and explained that he had been in communication with Mr Sergeant (of the SDR) on the subject, who proposed to advise his Directors to allow £100 by way of compensation on account of the use of the wires by the General Post Office - the Company to cede to the South Devon Co all present and future interest in the Telegraph. Mr Woollcombe (of the M&SDR) proceeded to contend that this company had no claim upon the Post Office for compensation, the Telegraph being virtually the property of the South

Devon Co, but stated that he was prepared to increase their offer to £150'.

The Route

The Moretonhampstead branch was single track and, as it rose some 500ft in its 12-odd miles, there were some stiff gradients, the steepest 1 in 49. Between Teigngrace and Bovey the line was laid partly on the route of the Haytor Tramway, a 7 mile horse-worked tramway which had opened in September 1820 to connect the quarries at Haytor Rock to the Stover Canal at Teigngrace. A distinctive feature of the tramway was that its tracks were made of granite blocks. These were each about 1ft 3in wide, and varied in length between 4ft and 8ft—the nominal gauge was 4ft 3in but, in marked contrast to later railway practice, the gauge narrowed on the curves. It has been suggested elsewhere that this is the reason why some sources refer to the '4ft gauge' Haytor Tramway.

The tramway, which was built by James Templar, is widely regarded as Devon's first railway, but that claim could be disputed by a timber-railed tramway and also a plateway, both in the Plymouth area, and dating from 1756 and 1812 respectively. The workings around Haytor fell into disuse in the 1850s through the availablity of cheaper granite from other quarries, and the tramway was abandoned in 1858. However, the durability of the granite tracks was such that many sections can still be clearly seen today. Some of the stone used in the construction of the National Gallery, the British Museum and London Bridge came from quarries at Haytor and, therefore, will have been transported over one of Devon's very first 'railways'.

On to more pertinent matters—the Moretonhampstead branch left the SDR's main line at Wolborough, on the northern outskirts of Newton Abbot, and originally had only two intermediate stations. The first was Bovey (6 miles and 6 chains from Newton Abbot station), which had two platforms, a crossing loop, and a substantial stone-built goods shed at the rear of the Up platform. Initially, Bovey station had the only signalbox on the branch other than the one at Moretonhampstead, but in 1882 a box at Chudleigh Road was added. The second station was at Lustleigh (8m 66ch), which had one platform and a short siding.

Other intermediate stopping places were added at Teigngrace (2m 28ch) in 1867, Chudleigh Road (3m 60ch) in 1874, Brimley Halt (5m 46ch) on 21 May 1928, and Hawkmoor Halt (7m 60ch) on 1 June 1931. Of those, Teigngrace was closed between 1 January 1917 and 1 May 1919, Chudleigh Road was renamed Heathfield on 1 October 1882, and Hawkmoor Halt was rechristened Pullabrook Halt on 13 June 1955.

The branch terminus at Moretonhampstead was a single plat-

Exeter-based 2-6-0 7316 waits at Platform 2 with a stopping train for Kingswear in July 1961. The engine ended its days at Exeter in September 1962. *Photograph R.S.Greenwood.*

branch, originally promoted under the banner of the Teign Valley Railway, was built to the standard gauge. The GWR's interest in the Teign Valley's 'out of gauge' corpse was not philanthropic as the old enemy, the L&SWR, was ready and waiting to step in. It appears that the GWR's accountants considered that a relatively minor expense was permissible if the L&SWR was to be kept out.

The Teign Valley branch was single track, and had a goods-only section beyond Ashton which was intended to serve local quarries and mines where a large-scale extraction of tin and copper had been planned. On 1 July 1903 it was joined end-on by a branch from Exeter, thereby providing a new, albeit localised, route between Exeter and Heathfield (formerly Chudleigh Road).

Although the Teign Valley branch through Ashton started at Heathfield, on the Moretonhampstead line, and was worked for much of its life largely as a separate entity, its story is too detailed to go into here. That said, the activities on the Teign Valley line had an effect on the comings and goings on part of the Moretonhampstead branch, with Newton Abbot - Christow goods workings a feature of the WTTs in the early days, and Newton Abbot - Heathfield - Exeter passenger workings appearing in the public timetables - for example, one each way in 1934 and 1940, two in 1943, 1944 and 1947, and one in 1955. Furthermore, the final Teign Valley branch public timetable (Winter 1957/58) reveals that three of the five daily trains each way ran through to or from Newton Abbot, and included some through workings to the Exe Valley line; for example, the 4.35pm ex-Newton Abbot worked through to Dulverton (arr. 6.58pm) and the 5.20pm from Tiverton ran to Newton Abbot (arr. 7.14pm).

After alterations were made to the

form affair with an all-over timber roof spanning part of the platform road and the run-round loop. The roof originally contained glazed sections, but they fell into disrepair and were ultimately replaced by corrugated iron sheeting in the 1950s. In its final form, the station yard accommodated a substantial stone-built goods shed, a cattle dock (alongside the dead end of the run round loop), and a single road engine shed built of stone with a slated roof. The shed, served from Newton Abbot, was built when the branch opened in 1866 and remained almost unaltered until its closure in November 1947. The brick-built station signal box (believed to be a post-1876 addition) was attached to the north wall of the engine shed. During the 1950s the overall impression of the station and its yard to this writer at least - was one of spa-

ciousness, in disproportion to the usual lack of activity.

In its later years, the branch had four private sidings - one to Messrs. Candy & Co at Heathfield, and others known as 'Pottery Siding', 'Granite Siding' and 'Electricity Siding'. Of these, the connection for Pottery Siding (which served a brick and tile works at Heathfield) had been passed by Colonel Rich for the Board of Trade on 19 April 1888. Interestingly, an earlier BOT inspection - by Colonel Yolland on 3 June 1873 - had reported on the connection of a siding between Lustleigh and Moretonhampstead, which had been laid 'for the clearance of Sandwick Wood'.

Chudleigh Road (Heathfield) station became a junction on 9 October 1882 when the GWR opened its 6.25 mile branch from that point to Ashton. The

Although Newton Abbot shed was covered in a recent BRILL we don't need any excuses for showing this splendid line-up taken in June 1954. *Photograph Rail Archive Stephenson.*

4-6-0 4905 BARTON HALL comes off shed at the west end of the station, the view probably being taken from platform 2. *Photograph Terry Nicholls.*

junction at Heathfield in 1916 to permit through working between Newton Abbot and the Teign Valley branch, the latter route became a useful alternative if the main line via Dawlish were blocked and was, in fact, only three quarters of a mile longer. However, the Teign Valley route was single track with just two passing places, and due to its sharp curves and steep gradients the largest locomotives normally permitted were '4500' class 2-6-2Ts. Furthermore, even the revised layout at Heathfield could not accommodate the passage of lengthy trains via the Ashton route, that matter being the subject of discussion in the May 1924 issue of the 'Railway Magazine'. An RM correspondent, Mr J.Brander of Bristol, explained that:

'Down trains over the Exeter Railway, after arriving at Heathfield Station, have to set back into a dead end siding and then start forward again to join the Teign Valley line to Newton Abbot.

'The length of this spur beyond the points leading to the Moretonhampstead line determines the length of the train that can be worked through without uncoupling.

'Heathfield Junction is one semi-island platform station; both lines are single except at some passing places, the Ashton and Exeter trains run into a short dead end, holding, at the most 6 'eights'. Passengers alight and walk across the

Table 8	SX	SO
Summer 1922	8	8
Winter 1934	9	9
Summer 1939	8	8
Winter 1940	7	8
Winter 1943	7	7
Winter 1944	7	8
Winter 1947	7	8
Summer 1955	9	9

outcome was that trains could then run through from Newton Abbot to Exeter via Heathfield and Ashton, as well as in the opposite direction.

After the unveiling of the new arrangements at Heathfield in 1927, the opening of the new halts at Brimley and Hawkmoor in 1928 and 1931 respectively, and the reduction of Teigngrace's status to that of a halt on 8 May 1939, the only significant cosmetic changes made to the Moretonhampstead branch during the rest of its life were the laying of a double junction (with the Teign Valley branch) at Heathfield in 1943, and the closure of Moretonhampstead engine shed in 1947.

Working the branch

During the early 1900s the normal pattern was for five passenger services each way on weekdays and two on Sundays, but the weekday services soon increased to eight in number. Looking at the WTT for July 1910, eight

These North British type 2s were the WR's diesel-hydraulic version of a NB diesel-electric class, the class-leader D6300 being seen piloting Castle 4-6-0 5058 EARL OF CLANCARTY at the head of a Plymouth-bound service from Newton Abbot, on 25 July 1959. *Photograph Terry Nicholls.*

platform to join the Newton - Moretonhampstead trains. The train could shunt back up the spur and then draw forward to the other side of the platform, but in the ordinary course of events there is no through traffic... The Down "Limited" ('Cornish Riviera') could be worked through by splitting and shunting in several portions, incidentally reversing the relative positions of some of the coaches, but the Up "Limited" would not manage at all.*

Matters at Heathfield were improved in 1927 when further alterations were made to the layout, these including the laying of a passing loop and a second platform for trains on the Moretonhampstead branch, and also the provision of a new signal box. The

trains are listed in each direction on weekdays with an additional service each way on Wednesday mornings. The Sunday service comprised two trains each way. One goods working in each direction was scheduled on weekdays (1.10pm ex-Newton, 4.25pm ex-Moreton) the return working being under instructions that wagons taken on at Lustleigh and Bovey were to be marshalled at Heathfield. Rolling stock for the passenger services usually took the form of four- or six-wheelers, but around 1911/12 a through carriage, an eight-wheeler it seems, to and from Paddington was advertised.

In later years, the numbers of passenger services advertised in the public timetables are given in table 8.

Moretonhampstead shed and signalbox, believed to have been photographed in the mid-1930s. The shed lost its sliding doors a couple of years after closure in November 1947 and the building was subsequently used by the Newton Abbot co-operative Society as a coal depot. The shed building still stands today, almost 47 years after closure. *Photograph W.A.Camwell.*

The branch timetables also included trains starting or terminating at Bovey (one each way in 1922, for example), and Newton Abbot - Heathfield workings which continued via the Teign Valley branch. Of the representative selection of timetables listed above, only the one for summer 1955 lists any Sunday services. These comprised four each way, of which two in each direction ran through to or from Torquay. The practice of trains originating or terminating at points beyond Newton Abbot was, however, certainly not ex-clusive to Sunday workings, the WTT for October 1947 to 30 May 1948 for example, revealing that one of the Down trains originated at Totnes and another at Paignton. That same WTT included one freight working each way on weekdays - 11.15am ex-Newton and 2.25 ex-Moreton.

The average journey times between Newton Abbot and Moretonhampstead in 1922 were 45 minutes Down and 35 minutes Up, those for 1955 being 35-40 minutes Down and 35 Up. The lengthier times for Down journeys re-flected the ascent in the direction of Moretonhampstead. The usual prac-tice - even after the closure of Moretonhampstead shed in 1947 - was for the last train of the day to work in the Down direction. Apart from the passenger services, the branch hosted a daily goods working throughout most of its existence.

Locomotives

After the branch was converted to the standard gauge in 1893 the usual steeds were the Wolverhampton-built '517' class 0-4-2Ts or Swindon's 'Metro' 2-4-0Ts, the '4500' class 2-6-2Ts ap-pearing not long after their introduc-tion in 1906. The freight workings were normally entrusted to 0-6-0ST/PTs.

The Swindon Registers reveal that the locomotives allocated to Moreton during 1909 were: 2-6-2T No 2173 (later renumbered 4512) until 27 Feb-ruary; 2-6-2T No 2179 (4518) 27 Feb-ruary to 24 April; 0-6-0ST No 1650 17 July to 8 September; 0-6-0ST No 1245 11 September to 9 October; 2-6-2T No 2182 (4521) 9 October for the rest of the year. Somewhat mysteriously, the Register reveals a takeover by 2-6-2Ts, No 4524 staying at Moreton shed un-til 25 April, followed by 4538 till the end of the year.

Auto-trains appeared on the line in the early 1930s, and eventually domi-nated proceedings. The archetypal lightweight GWR auto engines, the de-lightful little '4800' (later '1400') class 0-4-2Ts, are believed to have made their debut on the Moretonhampstad branch late in 1939, the first repre-sentative of the class—No 4866 - hav-ing been allocated to Newton Abbot shed on 25 February 1936. Starting on 8 February 1940, No 4827 (later renumbered 1427) became the regu-lar engine on the branch and, apart from a spell at Ashburton throughout 1948, retained that status until the closure of the line. No 1427, as it was then, finished its days at Cheltenham in June 1960.

By 21 March 1959 - less than three weeks after the closure of the Moretonhampstead branch—Newton Abbot's stud of 0-4-2Ts had been re-duced to three, Nos 1427 and 1472 (shown on the allocation lists for 15/5/1958) having, by then, been trans-ferred to Gloucester. For the record, selected GWR allocation lists for Moretonhampstead shed showed the residents to be 2-6-2T No 4504 in 9/1913, 4538 in 1/1921, No 4535 in 1/1934, and 0-4-2T No 1427 in 1/1947. Standard '3MT' 2-6-2Ts were used on the branch in the mid-1950s, but the crews were less than enamoured of the bunkers, smaller than the ex-GWR 2-6-2Ts which they were intended to re-place. The outcome was that the '3MTs' did not remain at Newton Abbot for very long.

During World War II the GWR-owned *Manor House Hotel* at Moretonhampstead was used as an army hospital, and special hospital

4803 at Moretonhampstead in June 1933. *Photograph Dr.Ian C.Allen.*

On the shortest - and possibly wettest - day of 1955, BR 3MT 2-6-2T 82032 prepares to leave Moretonhampstead with the 11.35 for Newton Abbot, 21 December 1955. These engines were not particularly popular with Newton Abbot crews, partly because their bunkers were smaller than those of the GWR 2-6-2Ts which they were intended to replace. The train formation consists of auto-trailers W224W and W234W. *Photograph Hugh Ballantyne.*

trains were operated via the Ashton line and Heathfield. Some untypical GWR locomotives, including 'Manor' 4-6-0s were permitted to use the line if necessary, but the most unusual form of motive power was, undoubtedly, the LNER 'B12' class 4-6-0s. During the war, at least eleven of them were allocated to ambulance train duties away from their home territory, their light axle-weights giving a usefully high route availability. The ambulance trains were based at Westbury, Newbury and Templecombe, the crew for each train comprising two drivers, two firemen, two guards and a resident Great Eastern Section fitter, all of whom lived on the train. Unfortunately, though, there seems to be an absence of records regarding which of the 'B12s' worked to Moretonhampstead.

By 1947 the WTTs noted that the engines permitted on the branch were 'blue' types: 4-6-0 78XX restricted to 20mph, other 'blue' types restricted to 25mph; all 'uncoloured' and 'yellow' but at Messrs. Candy & Co's siding at Heathfield, only 0-6-0T, 44xxs, 45xxs, 55xxs and 0-4-2Ts could work beyond the stop board, while at the Electricity Siding only 0-6-0Ts and 45/55XX 2-6-2Ts were permitted (but not beyond the stop board).

Etcetera

Throughout much of its life, the Moretonhampstead branch attracted a degree of seasonal passenger traffic. Among its publicised attractions during the early 1900s was a motor-bus service between Moretonhampstead and the village of Chagford. The GWR attempted to introduce a bus service to Chagford in 1905, but the county council refused to foot the bill for the necessary road improvements. With commendable persistence, the GWR did further battle with the authorities, and road improvements were made in time for the bus service to commence on 14 April 1906. Two vehicles were used on that route, with two others on the Moretonhampstead - Princetown route, inaugurated in July 1909.

A well-known feature of the branch was the 'Visitors Book' at Lustleigh station. The famed book was the subject of an article in the 'GWR Magazine' of July 1923:

'To the station master at Lustleigh, Mr F.J.Haywood, is due the credit for having introduced a book in the station waiting room for the reception of the views and opinions of visitors respecting the attractions of this beauty spot in the "Shire of the Sea Kings". The idea is a happy one which might with advantage be followed at other places.

'Started in 1916, the book contains the tributes of visitors from far and near, e.g. Canada, Jamaica and Nigeria, besides a host of testimonies from numerous English holidaymakers who flocked to the West of England for their vacations during the time when air raids were not unknown elsewhere in our country.

'The wealth of praise of the beauties of the Lustleigh surroundings contained between the covers of this volume would do credit to the most eulogistic verbosity of a guide-book writer, and it is doubtful if any adjective suggesting the "delectable", "exquisite", "beautiful" or "picturesque" has been omitted. Whilst not a few of the writings are in humourous vein and some border on the cynical, the general effect is a record of genuine appreciation of the unique

charms of this "Corner of God's Garden", as one visitor describes it.

'In one instance, a testimony to the natural beauty of the locality is linked with a request for more "houses of public refreshment" (the editor of BRILL must have been a mere teenager when he wrote THAT in the visitors' book) and another shows the mixed mentality of the writer who, after exhausting his vocabulary in praise of Nature's handiwork, suggested, if you please, that a "good picture show" would be a desirable acquisition.

'There are, of course, frequent references to The Cleave, Becky Falls, the Bullaton and Nutcracker Rocks; and "the Old Cottage" comes in for its measure of adulation. These laudations are, however, not entirely limited to the scenery, for visitors to Lustleigh also bear written tribute of their appreciation of the station, the station garden, and the station staff. It would appear that the Goth and the Hun have also had access to the visitors' book, for here and there one finds passages which have been blacked out or otherwise deleted by the better-minded, who have added their words of censure.

'Among others, a scholar from New York has been here and left his appreciation in Greek characters, and the next contributor has recorded in no ambiguous words his views on such pedantry. Here is variety, for whilst the following is contributed by a visitor from California U.S.A: "Beautiful Devon! Home of our ancestors. Almost equal to our Southern California", on the next page we have an admission that "Lustleigh is a lot better than Landore"'.

The Moretonhampstead branch also featured in the 'GWR Magazine' of January 1938 (cover price One Penny!), the subject this time being a Royal tour which left London on 30 November the previous year and included a jaunt to Moretonhampstead:

'The Royal train used throughout the tour consisted of ten coaches, including the King's saloon, dining and sleeping saloons, and was drawn by the "Windsor Castle" locomotive, which was used throughout the tour for all the main line journeys. The engine carried the Royal Arms and "Crown" head lamps throughout and was wired for telephone communication with the train.

'King George VI is the first reigning monarch to travel over the branch line from Newton Abbot, and when he stepped off the train at Moretonhampstead at 10.15am on Wednesday December 1st, hundreds of school children in the station yard, armed with Union Jacks and lusty voices, gave him a sample of the enthusiastic welcome which was accorded him throughout the tour.

'The first day's road tour was from Moretonhampstead, across Dartmoor to Princetown, Tavistock and Launceston, the Duchy's ancient capital'.

In 1934 one of the first wave of GWR

camping coaches was installed at Lustleigh. The announcement that the GWR had followed the LNER's lead in this novel field came a shade belatedly in the 'GWR Magazine' of October 1934. The article enthused that:

'Comfort and convenience are outstanding characteristics of the plan and fitting of these coaches. The six-berth coach comprises one 2-berth and one 4-berth sleeping compartment. The beds in the former represent the long and comfortably-sprung compartment seats, while in the latter, two overhead suspended berths have been added. There is an ample provision of blankets, rugs, sheets, pillows and pillow linen, so that the utmost sleeping comfort is assured.

'The remaining portion of the coach is devoted to day-time accommodation. This comprises a roomy dining room, equipped with a table, six chairs, and a wardrobe. The dining-room gives access to the kitchen, which is fitted with the utmost convenience and compactness, with a Primus stove and oven, a table, with cupboard below, a sink, and a draining board'.

The GWR's charges for its camping coaches were, at first, £3 per week for the six-berth type and £5 per week for the ten-berth version. A condition of letting was that the hirers had to purchase monthly return tickets from their home station, four tickets being necessary for those hiring six-berth coaches and six tickets for hirers of the ten-berth vehicles.

British Railways
Inevitably, the increase in car owner ship in the 1950s had its effect on the Moretonhampstead branch. In November 1955 British Railways published an in-depth report on the state of play of the railways of Devon and Cornwall, and the conclusion was that most of the branch lines were not just ailing, but terminally ill. The report was based on the traffic figures for the period October 1954 to May 1955, the latter date - as has been pointed out by Michael Harris, who unearthed the relevant document at the Public Record Office and wrote about it in *Steam Days* magazine earlier this year - covering the footplatmen's two-week strike which effectively resulted in much of BR's freight traffic being irretrievably lost to the roads.

The figures quoted for the Moretonhampstead branch revealed that, during the period under scrutiny, the average number of local passengers using the branch (i.e: excluding those travelling beyond Newton Abbot) was just 87 each weekday. Freight traffic comprised some 200-270 full wagon loads inwards each month, with between 171 and 264 wagons being dispatched. The bottom line was that the revenue from the branch amounted to £7,637 while the working expenses (excluding trainmen's wages) were £10,088.

During a trip on the branch on Thursday 7 August 1958, local railway

The last day of passenger services on the Moretonhampstead branch was 28 February 1959 and, true to form, BRILL finds the man who was present to photograph 2-6-2T 4117 working the 14.15 ex Newton Abbot after arriving at Moretonhampstead for the last time. *Photograph Terry Nicholls.*

historian (and avid BRILL reader) Mr Eric Youldon travelled on the 2.15pm from Newton Abbot and returned on the 3.15pm from Moretonhampstead, the engine being 0-4-2T No 1427. The number of passengers joining and leaving are shown in table 9.

Mr Youldon remarks that the weather on the day was fine, and although he travelled during a quiet part of the day he emphasises that, at the time, the holiday season was in full swing. Taking seasonal trends into account, his findings reflect the figures quoted by British Railways just three years earlier.

The line's status as an archetypal ex-GWR country branch was, of course, of no commercial value, and the outcome was that passenger services were withdrawn as from 2 March 1959. The branch remained open for freight until April 1964 when the section above Bovey was closed completely. The remains of the branch were further truncated in July 1970 when the section above Heathfield oil terminal was closed completely. The section serving the oil terminal (about half a mile beyond the site of Heathfield station) nevertheless remains in use to

this day, one train of tank wagons hauled by a 'Class 60' diesel arriving from Waterston each Tuesday.

As a footnote, the Heathfield - Ashton - Exeter (Teign Valley) branch, to which considerable reference has been made, lost its passenger services on 9 June 1958, its status as an alternative route for main line traffic having been finally negated by the Western Region's inheritance of the ex-L&SWR Exeter - Okehampton - Plymouth route. The WR and, before it, the GWR, had, in fact, favoured the SR's Okehampton route as an alternative since the early 1940s, and so the Teign Valley branch had, since then, had only a nominal existence as an alternative route for main line traffic.

Other uncredited sources: *Railways of Devon* (Martin Smith); *The Great Western in South Devon* (Keith Beck & John Copsey).

Acknowledgement: Sincere thanks are due to Mr Bill Peto of the Great Western Society and to Mr Eric Youldon of Exeter for their invaluable assistance and advice during the preparation of this article.